TEACHING AS

JESUS TAUGHT

By

John Garlock

GOSPEL PUBLISHING HOUSE
Springfield, Missouri 65802

2-615

This is a Workers Training Division
textbook. Credit for its study will be
issued under Classification Four.
NATIONAL SUNDAY SCHOOL DEPARTMENT,
ASSEMBLIES OF GOD

CONTENTS

INTRODUCTION

If you are a Sunday school teacher, this book is especially for you. If you are not a Sunday school teacher, you should imagine yourself one as you study the book.

While it is my hope that much of what is said here may be of benefit to anyone who is actively engaged in other gospel work, it is also my conviction that most kinds of "active gospel work" involve some sort of teaching activity. This is true of pastors, assistants, youth leaders, gospel musicians, administrators, and secretaries just as it is of Sunday school teachers themselves. But in a way, the Sunday school teacher is the epitome of method in Christian education of the twentieth century. For that reason this book is addressed principally and without equivocation to the Sunday school teacher.

Further, the book assumes that most of the Sunday school teachers to whom it is addressed have already had some teaching experience. They know something of the joys—and the frustrations—of teaching the Christian gospel. They have already faced and wrestled with many of the problems which are the framework of this book. If you are such a teacher, you will be able to relate quickly to the challenges and dilemmas with which the following pages are concerned.

Those who study this book in a workers training

course have widely varying interests. Some will take it up in the hope that it will turn out to be a study of the life of Christ. Others will wish it were an outline of New Testament doctrines based upon the teachings of Christ. Many would prefer it to be purely a devotional study. Still others will be looking for a textbook of teaching methods. All will be disappointed, for the book is none of these. *Teaching as Jesus Taught* is basically a review of ten important situations every Sunday school teacher faces.

But is such an approach Biblical enough? To be strictly "Biblical," a book should start with the truths of the Bible and proceed to relate them to human life and work. However, the attempt to proceed this way often leads into inpenetrable and tangled swamps indeed, for no limit can ever be found to the extent of Biblical truth. Books which pride themselves on being "Biblical" therefore often end up as selective commentaries—offering helpful remarks about some Bible truth while ignoring other equally important Bible truth.

A lifetime of careful, dedicated teaching could never convey *all* the truth. Obviously, the teaching process requires selective choice. Some of the choice is made by the planners of curriculum, some by the teacher himself. All too often his selections are based upon what is easiest to prepare, or what he feels most at home discussing. He is naturally tempted to avoid areas about which he is not sure, or which will raise difficult and possibly embarrassing questions.

Imagine a fully equipped and sumptuous restaurant, but one which has no menu from which its patrons may select their own meals. Rather, the cook is free to serve whatever he wishes. Though the kitchen and storerooms may contain the widest possible variety of fine foods, including everything needed for nutritional balance, is it not likely that the diners will end up receiving those dishes the cook most likes to prepare? In fact, however hardworking he may be, the cook's own habits and predispositions may cause him to prepare the same few dishes over and over and over again. They may be masterpieces but still fall far short of giving a true indication of the scope and variety the resources of the restaurant could provide. What is more serious, the chef's specialties may not match the actual nutritional needs of those who come for food.

A teacher is in a comparable position. The chapters of this book are designed to help him overcome his personal bias by showing how a few of the more difficult but necessary dishes may be prepared. May our spiritual cooking skills increase and our vitamins abound!

The late W. I. Evans of Central Bible College was fond of saying, "The truth usually lies somewhere between two extremes." Clearly or vaguely, most of us are aware of this. More often than not, the best position may be one of balance, taking into account the dangers of overstating one truth or the other. For instance, to exaggerate the insecurity of a believer's position before God is just as great a mistake as to exaggerate the believer's security.

However, it is a mistake to think that the truth necessarily lies exactly halfway between the two extremes each and every time. In fact there will be times when the truth lies very close to one extreme or the other. For example, man has responsibilities to himself and also responsibilities to God. Either of these responsibilities can be stated in extreme terms. But it is much nearer the Christian position to say that a man should live "completely" for God than to say he should live "completely" for himself. In this and many other cases the truth is *not* found in a balanced compromise between the two extremes.

Keep this in mind as you read this book. Each chapter is based upon a kind of polarity of two ideas, either of which may be stated in extreme terms. In some cases the one view should receive greater emphasis than the other; in other cases both are of fairly equal value. For example, chapter 4 attempts to show that it is important to make teaching attractive, but also important to make it contain what pupils need. In good teaching these are in fairly equal balance. However, in chapter 10 the intent is to show that "to impart" is a highly inadequate view of the teaching process; "to implant" is finer, more lasting, and more Christian. There is no attempt to present these concepts in equal balance.

Teaching as Jesus Taught starts at the application end rather than the origin end of the truth. It takes ten basic situations—or, if you prefer, problems— which every Christian teacher inevitably faces; it then attempts to give guidance in the handling of these problems, using direct examples from the life and teaching of our Lord. Without apology, the starting point is the problems of the teacher. But these problems are much closer to being "Biblical" than many people might think—for Jesus Himself was primarily a teacher. When we examine the problems of the Christian teacher, therefore, we are also examining the problems which Jesus Himself faced as He taught men the truth that could make them free.

Of each of the questions faced in the chapters of this book it can be said that:

1. Jesus faced the question.
2. Today's Christian teacher also faces it.
3. The question can most effectively be dealt with by applying today the principles Jesus used in His time.

Of course, each such problem is actually a whole cluster of smaller, related problems. And it is unlikely that even the smallest of them is answered adequately in this book. I must be content with pointing to Christ, the all-time master teacher, in such a way as to bring anew before today's teachers the power of His perception, His dedication, His methods, His example.

In an inspirational or devotional sense, the purpose of this book is to help teachers identify with Christ Himself. He who teaches others the truth cannot but be filled with reverence and wonder when he realizes that his efforts, however small, place him in the same occupation—and with the same eternal goals—as Jesus Christ.

Ever since education became recognized as a science, it has been customary to analyze the *content* of teaching quite separately from the *method* of teaching. This is a useful convenience. However, the more closely blended are the content and the method employed, the more successful the teaching is likely to be. In Christ's story of the prodigal son (Luke 15:11-32), for instance, the story is so closely identified with the truth of forgiveness that the story virtually *becomes* the doctrine of forgiveness. Perhaps this blend of content and method came more easily in the unscientific society of Jesus' day. But it is nevertheless true that the average Sunday school teacher, in the average Sunday school teaching situation, blends content and method often and repeatedly—*and should.*

If this book has any•claim to novelty (among the hundreds of books which have been written on the general subject of teaching methods and the teachings of Jesus) it is in the fact that it deliberately attempts to bridge the gap between content and method and blend the two. Each of the basic principles dealt with— one in each of the ten chapters—is a principle that has implications both for *what* a teacher teaches and *how* he teaches it.

Christ's own teaching was always live, personal, immediate; He never taught merely through words or by remote control. His very life and His teachings were inseparably blended. It was impossible for anyone to separate *what* He taught from the *way* He taught it or from what He *was*. The closer today's teacher can come to this ideal, the more nearly he will succeed in teaching as Jesus taught.

—1—
TEACHING OR PREACHING?

Preaching at its noblest has been called the manifestation of the *living Word* (Christ) through the *written Word* (Scripture) by the *spoken word* (the utterance of the preacher). Yet this definition would apply equally well not only to Christian *preaching* at its best but also to Christian *teaching* at its best. For we all know there can be a considerable amount of overlap between the two. After a particularly evangelistic type of Sunday school lesson a pupil may say to his teacher, "That was a fine bit of gospel preaching!" Or when an evangelist has led his congregation safely through a maze of complex prophetic exposition, you may go up to him afterward, shake his hand, and say, "I certainly appreciated your Bible teaching tonight!"

There are significant differences between teaching and preaching, as we shall soon see. However, there are also distinct ways in which the two are similar— sometimes so similar as to be nearly identical. Teacher, whether you realize it or not, you have probably done a good bit of preaching in your time!

SIMILARITIES

Preaching and teaching are similar in the following ways:

1. Both should be based solidly upon the Bible.
2. Both should have evangelism as a main goal.

3. Both require the anointing of the Holy Spirit to be truly effective.

4. Both require sound techniques of communication.

5. Both are most effective only when the communicator is thoroughly dedicated to his task.

DIFFERENCES

Then do preaching and teaching mean the same thing? No. Some people feel that a Sunday school teacher is really just a preacher for one particular age group, usually working in a smaller auditorium. This is far too limited a view of Christian teaching. Despite the overlapping, the two forms of communication are generally different in at least two important respects. Here are the differences:

1. Teaching is not as limited to the spoken word as preaching is. That is, a teacher communicates by a wider range of methods than does the average preacher. For example, the teacher is much more likely to use visual aids, discussions, questions and answers, or group projects than is a preacher. There are several reasons for this. The most obvious in most churches is that teaching generally takes place in much smaller groups than preaching does. The preacher tends to be more limited to the spoken word as a method.

2. Teaching (as compared with preaching) usually has a long-term, continuative character. It is not concerned with just a lesson, but with a whole progression of related lessons. Teaching takes the long view. It is concerned with a process; it repeats and interlocks its truths; it has a serial, scheduled quality.

There are other possible differences between teaching and preaching, but the above-mentioned two are the main ones. You may be surprised not to see a longer list of differences. For example, you may feel that one of the chief differences between teaching and preaching is in the emotional tone of the communicator's presentation. It is true this is often a difference, but it is not a *necessary* difference. Is teaching often drier? It doesn't have to be! Is preaching more fiery and inspired? Teaching can also be fiery and inspired! Does preaching seem to move the hearts of people more? The right kind of teaching can move people's hearts just as much. We teachers can learn a great deal from gospel preachers, yet without fear of encroaching upon their territory. They are the proclaimers; we are the explainers. And our field is far broader than most of us take advantage of.

A COMBINATION

Jesus Himself was both preacher and teacher. Near the beginning of His ministry He quoted and applied to Himself the words of Isaiah, " ... He hath anointed me to preach ... " (Isaiah 61:1; Luke 4:18). Nevertheless, most of the people among whom He lived and worked recognized His occupation as that of teacher. Nicodemus, for instance, came to Him saying, "We know that thou art a teacher come from God ... " (John 3:2).

It is a thrill to realize that this puts the Christian teacher in a special relationship to the Lord Jesus Christ. As teachers of His Word, we share in what was His most pronounced occupation. With Him, we are teachers of the truth, and we should be glad to share with Him in this special way.

A teacher also has a special relationship to the Christian church. He helps to pass along, to perpetuate the values, attitudes, and activities which have made

the church of Jesus Christ a living, dynamic thing
through the centuries. Despite its divine origin, without teachers the church would die.

TEACHING AND EVANGELISM

When Jesus commissioned His pupils to "Go . . .
teach all nations" (Matthew 28:19), He recognized the
continuous as well as the instantaneous aspect of evangelism. It is doubtful if many people have become
Christians as the result of hearing one lone gospel
sermon—with no preparation of heart and mind by
teaching. Even in such spectacular scriptural cases as
those of the Ethiopian eunuch (Acts 8:26-40), the
household of Cornelius (Acts 10), and the Philippian
jailer (Acts 16:25-34), it seems that hearts had been in
the process of preparation for some time. And the
preparation was a teaching-study-learning process.

Picture the building of a great solid pyramid. Let
the base of the pyramid represent teaching; let the
height represent inspirational preaching. It is easy
to see that a basic foundation must be laid before any
height can be attained. It is also easy to see that
the higher the pinnacle, the broader the base necessary
to support it. So is teaching related to preaching. A
solid structure will have proportioned increase in both
dimensions.

THE TEACHER'S VIEWPOINT

Jesus looked at His own teaching in three ways—
ways which can be helpful to every Christian teacher
today. He saw teaching as:

1. Partly preaching (e.g., His quotation of Isaiah in
the Nazareth synagogue, Luke 4:18).

2. Continuative even beyond His personal ministry

(e.g., the Great Commission, Matthew 28:18-20) .

3. Specialized in those committed to His care (e.g., John 14 and 15) .

All three of these are healthy ways of looking at teaching. Whatever the age level you teach, you should see yourself as partly a preacher. You should proclaim, announce, stir, appeal to your hearers.

Yet you should also have the long view, looking beyond your own lifetime to the results of the character-building you are doing today. American poetess Emily Dickinson has written:

> "A word is dead
> When it is said,
> Some say.
> I say it just
> Begins to live
> That day."

As teacher you should also see your influence as concentrated in those who are learning from you. Do you feel insignificant in the great kingdom of God? Do you feel that even in your own church you can have little influence on the congregation? Take heart! When you are with your own Sunday school class in the privacy and sanctity of your own appointed place of teaching—be it bare or luxurious—your opportunity for influence is tremendous. Specialize here, where your power is greatest. A few lives well-trained will make a greater mark upon the world than many lives barely touched.

METHODS

Earlier it was noted that one of the distinctive features of teaching is the wide variety of methods available to the teacher. That is, the teacher may and should do more than just talk. It is not our purpose to make a detailed analysis of all the methods available to the teacher, but a brief mention of the principal ones may be helpful.

1. *The lecture method.* This is the oldest and most widely used of all teaching methods. Of all methods, it can probably present the greatest amount of material in the shortest space of time. It is also more likely to stay on the subject than are some of the methods which make use of wider participation. However, it is probably capable of being the driest of all teaching methods when employed by an unenthusiastic and inexpert teacher. It may be greatly enlivened by the use of audio-visual aids—as may many of the other methods.

2. *The question-and-answer method.* This is great for stimulating the thinking of pupils—provided you ask the right kind of questions. It is usually impossible to plan a complete list of questions ahead of time, as you cannot know what pupils' answers will be. Therefore this method can often be very frustrating for the teacher—and hence for pupils as well. But it has the advantage of offering pupils the opportunity for direct and immediate response.

3. *Discussion or debate.* These methods are particularly applicable to subject matter that deals with two opposite but fairly balanced points of view. For *discussion,* no one should begin by expressing a positive conclusion. The emphasis is upon group thinking and the attempt to progress together toward fuller understanding. In *debate,* each side has a committed position to defend, and presents every possible point in favor of its assigned point of view.

4. *The assignment and report method.* This method

is particularly useful where a class contains persons who are themselves capable of useful teaching. Each member of the class in turn prepares and presents factual, devotional, or other material coordinated with lesson subjects. The class learns; and the student teacher learns most of all.

5. *The project method.* This consists of work activity which may be done separately by each individual or by the group as a whole. Some projects, such as a marked map or a miniature ark of the covenant, may be prepared in class to form part of the equipment of the classroom. Other projects may be completed by individuals or pairs of pupils as homework. Generally, the younger the age group, the more tangible and physical the project should be. More advanced ages may prefer research or paper-work projects.

6. *The role-playing method.* This is one of the newer techniques, and one with which very few teachers feel at home. However, it has great possibilities for all age groups—if your class can overcome shyness and inhibitions. The idea is to have members of the class act out a problem situation related to the lesson material. No dialogue is memorized, and a minimum of instruction should be given the role players. Rather, they should attempt simply to feel the emotions of the real-life persons they represent. The purpose is not to present entertaining drama, but to give members of a class the opportunity to experience vicariously the feelings of other people. The participants themselves learn most.

7. *The field trip method.* This is hardly practical during a Sunday school hour. However, a teacher can easily use this method as a supplementary device for giving reality to a subject. For example, a teacher

may add vividness to the study of the problems of the underprivileged by arranging a Saturday class trip to a jail, an orphanage, or a welfare office.

THE TEACHING SITUATION

Herman Harrell Horne, in his book *Jesus, the Master Teacher,* points out that any teaching situation always contains at least six basic considerations. In somewhat adapted form they are as follows:

1. One or more teachers.
2. One or more pupils.
3. An environment (the physical circumstances where the teaching takes place).
4. A curriculum (the material or "lesson" taught).
5. One or more aims (the purpose or result toward which the teacher is working).
6. One or more methods (the means used to achieve the aims).

Perhaps the best-known teaching situation in the New Testament is the story of Jesus and the woman at the well of Samaria (John 4). Obviously, the teacher was Jesus, the pupil was the woman. Read through the chapter and see if you can make a few accurate remarks about the environment, the curriculum, the aim, and the method.

You may notice that Jesus' teaching method in this story is difficult to identify in terms of the modern methods we have been describing. In your own teaching, too, you probably could not describe what happens in any given class period as being all one method or another. A teacher frequently blends, combines, shifts, or adapts methods to meet circumstances. And there are some teaching techniques which are more matters of viewpoint or approach than they are matters of actual procedure. In the woman-at-the-well situation, Jesus took advantage of such factors as these:

Occasion—capitalizing on the special opportunity offered by circumstances.

Point of contact—the opening request, "Give me to drink."

Attention and interest—the startling fact of a Jew speaking to a Samaritan woman in a public place.

Conversational method—the naturalness with which the exchange of ideas moved forward.

Individual tutoring—the contact with one person as a means of reaching many.

Person-to-person relationship—making the experience a face-to-face encounter rather than a detached academic experience.

Answering questions—responding to and building upon what the woman asked Him.

Approach through problems—dealing with "where should God be worshiped?"

Apperception (connecting new truth with old) —the progression from a reference to water to a reference to *living* water.

The concrete—reference to the specific: "This water . . . ," "This mountain . . . "

Imagery by contrast—comparison of the views of the Samaritans with those of the Jews; the difference between two kinds of water.

Personal motivation—the appeal to the woman's *interests,* to her *conscience,* to her desire for *service* (calling others) .

Opportunity for response—"Go, call thy husband . . . "[1]

One of the best definitions of education calls it

---

[1] Adapted from an analysis by Horne, *op. cit.*, pp. 4-7

"guided experience." This is simply a short way of saying that experience is not merely the *best* teacher— it is actually the *only* teacher. It is just that experience is of two kinds: that which comes to the pupil *personally,* and that which comes to him *vicariously—* such as the experience of others he reads about.

THE TEACHER AS ORGANIZER

Unless a person plans otherwise, the life experiences that come to him are more or less at random. They may occur in a vast variety of sequences, and sometimes in ways that prevent him from getting the most out of them. When we say that education is "guided experience," we mean that a *control* has been introduced in order that the experiences which come to the pupil will come in an order and at a rate which will make it possible for him to gain most from them. Normally, the one guiding the experience is the teacher. However, it is possible for mature individuals to give themselves a certain amount of education by exercising their own guidance over (or control of) the sequence of experiences life brings.

All of this is a slightly complex way of saying that a teacher should not merely *let* things happen; a good teacher *makes* things happen. He exercises guidance and control with a definite purpose in view.

One may think of good teaching as consisting of two things:

1. Having something worthwhile to teach.
2. Getting results in teaching it.

Remember, we are interested in results, not merely in attempts. An old adage says, "If the pupil hasn't learned, the teacher hasn't taught." Think it over. It is uncomfortably true.

MEANS AND ENDS

However, this presents a strong temptation to assume that in teaching, "the end justifies the means"—that any method is legitimate as long as it obtains the desired results. But again it is necessary to recall the inseparability of content and method in Christian teaching. God's ultimate embodiment of the truth was in a person—Jesus Christ. And Christ's ultimate embodiment of His gospel is also in persons—Christian teachers. Therefore they have more than a mere responsibility to convey facts in whatever way may happen to work. They must also communicate spirit, character, faith, love—all the things that make up the truth of the Christian life. Jesus Himself never for a moment did or said anything which would imply, "Do as I say, not as I do." His teaching permeated His life. So should yours and mine.

Early in the chapter it was mentioned that the second important differentiating characteristic of teaching (as compared with preaching) is its long-term continuative character. Teaching is always a stick-with-it kind of job. It can rarely if ever be a "one-shot" effort. What are some of the implications?

1. A teacher must be patient.

2. A teacher must be regular in attendance.

3. A teacher's vision must extend beyond one lesson; he must see a quarter or a year at a time.

Many of the principles of good Christian teaching would apply to any kind of teaching, Christian or not. And it is perfectly true that education in general— even quite secular education—can teach valuable items of truth. The great plus factor of *Christian* education is that it teaches people not only to know truth, but to know *the Truth,* the one who is the embodiment of all that is true in the highest sense. And in Christian teaching this plus factor should always be present. Never be satisfied to have your pupils handling mere facts, however well they do it. Strive until each is touching God for himself.

QUESTIONS

1. Describe two important ways in which teaching is different from preaching.

2. Answer "preaching" or "teaching" to each of the following: Which more frequently has the more emotional tone? Which usually takes the longer range view? Which uses the greater variety of methods? Which is likelier to address larger groups of people? Which was Jesus' more pronounced occupation?

3. What is the most widely used teaching method?

4. What is the difference between discussion and debate?

5. What is meant by "curriculum"?

6. What is meant by "apperception"?

7. What is the best known teaching situation where Jesus worked with an individual, and where is the story found?

8. Explain the idea, "Experience is the *only* teacher."

9. What is the formal word for "guided experience"?

10. Explain the statement, "People are not converted by hearing one lone sermon."

11. Explain the statement, "A teacher is partly a preacher."

—2—

THE OLD OR THE NEW?

The teacher of a boys class faced the group a little nervously because it was his first Sunday with them. "Now that we've all found the place in our Bibles," he said, "we'll have Jimmy here read the story aloud while the rest of us follow along silently. All right, Jimmy..."

Suddenly one of the boys put up his hand. When called upon he said, "But that's not the way Brother Johnson used to do. *He* always had each of us read just one verse, then it was the next fellow's turn."

Have you ever had this sort of thing happen in a class you teach? Sometimes it is amazing how much a class has been impressed by "how our other teacher did it." And it often seems that pupils are much more likely to remember *how* their lessons were taught than *what* was actually communicated.

Unless the teacher who preceded you was really pretty bad, there are sure to be some in your class who have become well adjusted to and very satisfied with his ways. And they just wish you would carry on in the same manner and not rock the boat. "But Mrs. Thompson said we should never do that." "But for years we've always had the picnic at the municipal park." "Well, always before we had the boys sit on the *left* side." The possible examples are endless. Pupils— and often teachers too—may get very disturbed when someone changes the system they are used to.

It may be helpful for each of us to examine his attitudes with regard to new ways versus old. Your attitude toward change can reveal a great deal about your work as a teacher.

TWO OPPOSITE PRINCIPLES

God has made a universe in which the principle of change and the principle of changelessness are both continually present and operative. He delights in the creation of what is new, fresh, and different—yet there are some features of nature which seem always the same. Many a man has taken comfort from the changelessness of the stars, the sea, or some familiar mountain. Yet scientifically, of course, all of these are also changing continuously. It is just that their cycle of changes may be so very long as compared with human life that they seem to remain eternally in one condition.

FOUR VIEWPOINTS

1. *The Revolutionary Viewpoint.* This is an attitude of extreme dissatisfaction with things as they are, coupled with a determination to bring about a drastic change. Of course a person may be a revolutionary in his views of, say, art—while at the same time being perfectly satisfied with conditions in the field of politics. That is, a revolutionary is not necessarily a revolutionary about everything.

Specifically, a revolutionary is one who is so dissatisfied about a certain set of conditions that he believes the only cure is a sudden and radical change of those conditions. He tends to favor a kind of "overthrow" of an existing pattern, and the substitution of a new or totally altered one.

Some commentators on the life and work of Jesus are fond of referring to Him as a revolutionary. And He has been considered such by a great many people—both those of His own time and others down through the centuries. From one point of view, He *was* certainly very much a revolutionary. The Son of God came to earth to alter—drastically and suddenly—the whole basis of relationship between God and man. You could say He was very much dissatisfied with "things as they were" and inaugurated wide and sweeping changes.

However, it is important to point out that in most ways Jesus was *not* a revolutionary in the political or social sense. He did not advocate the forcible overthrow of any government, social structure, or religious organization. This despite the fact that all these things certainly needed great changes in His time.

2. *The Progressive Viewpoint.* The person with this attitude is also dissatisfied with things as they are (the status quo) and wants to see changes made. But, unlike the revolutionary, he does not think these changes should necessarily be sudden and radical. The progressive leans more toward a steady, step-by-step change in the desired direction.

Some progressives may have a tendency to confuse change with progress. They may act as if some automatic process is at work that will make things get better and better if people are just kept moving. They tend to think the newest way is sure to be the best.

In its highest form, the progressive viewpoint seems to be the one God Himself has taken with regard to His revelation of divine truth to man. The incarnation of Christ was the ultimate step in a long, progressive series of heavenly communications (Hebrews 1:1).

3. *The Conservative Viewpoint.* Conservatives often tend to resist change. They are not categorically against it, but are very wary of making changes unless they are perfectly sure that the change is necessary. As with the word *revolutionary,* the term *conservative* may be applied to a vast number of fields of human activity. A person may be a conservative in one way but not in another.

Conservatism values time-honored viewpoints and methods. It feels that what has worked well in the past should be respected, held on to, or "conserved." Jesus demonstrated considerable conservatism in His life and ministry by His great respect for Moses and the prophets. He often made it clear that there were many things in the Old Testament patterns that He felt were worth preserving.

4. *The Reactionary Viewpoint.* This view not only is opposed to changing the status quo, but insists that too much change has *already* taken place. The reactionary is so called because he "reacts" against efforts to bring change. He does not initiate; rather he fights back at those who do. Whatever the area of his reactionism, he tends to long for the "good old days." Of the four views here listed, reactionism is the one of which the fewest traces appear in the ministry of Jesus.

The terms, *revolutionary, progressive, conservative,* and *reactionary* are used above only as to their meanings regarding attitude toward change. The words often mean something else when used in other areas of thought. For example, "conservative" in a theological sense has come to mean those doctrines and attitudes which fully accept the deity of Christ, the inspiration of Scripture, the reality of the supernatural, and other doctrines which have been basic to the Christian church through the centuries. The Assemblies of God is a conservative fellowship. Of course this meaning is not unrelated to the meaning of *conservative* when used as a description of an attitude that is somewhat suspicious of change. We believe that fundamental doctrines should not change, but methods perhaps will.

A QUESTION FOR ALL TEACHERS

Though the problems of a Sunday school teacher are quite different in many respects from those of a teacher in a public school system, they have enough in common that it may be worthwhile to consider the great division of emphasis that exists in the thinking of teachers throughout the world.

Anthropologists tell us that some form of education exists in all societies—though it may not be formalized by books and schoolrooms. Among primitive tribal peoples, the teaching of children is thought of as consisting entirely of passing on to them the existing values and skills of their elders. There is very little awareness of any forward movement of technology or social patterns. Education is strictly a "handing down" procedure. The teacher is not expected to evaluate, alter, adapt, or improve. His work is simply to perpetuate what is already known or believed.

The more civilized societies (keeping in mind that they are not necessarily more Christian) are always inclined to give teachers a greater scope for innovation. In such societies teachers are more likely to consider education as the attempt to achieve the highest level of understanding—whether it is what the society already believes or not. This means that in cultures such as ours in America, schools are not necessarily striving to teach our children the values and skills of their parents. For the educators may well believe that the parents' system is quite wrong. It is no secret that some of the strongest critics of the American way of life have deliberately sought teaching positions. They know that in this way they have the greatest opportunity to change that way of life—which is precisely their purpose.

The "perpetuation of knowledge" view of education runs the continual risk of becoming stale and irrelevant to current life. Yet the "find the truth" view, in its extreme form, inevitably means a kind of ceaseless experimentation.

SUNDAY SCHOOL SIGNIFICANCE

How does all this affect the teacher in the Sunday school? Actually each of the extremes of viewpoint described above has its counterpart in religious education—complete with comparable dangers.

But there is a great and important difference between secular education and Christian education which has a direct bearing on the subject. If in Sunday school we are teaching the Bible, and if the Bible is God's Word, and if God's Word is essentially changeless—then the Sunday school teacher should strenuously resist change. By contrast, teachers of secular subjects are conveying the knowledge of mere men, which to say the least is far from changeless. This basic difference, besides any other factors, will tend to make a good Sunday school teacher much more conservative in approach than a good public school teacher.

WHEN CHANGE IS GOOD

There are nevertheless many changes toward which

the Sunday school teacher should be alert and receptive. For one thing, not all of the heritage passed down to us is always solidly based on the Bible. Changes that would line up these traditions with the Scripture are very much in order.

For another thing, the *application* of a spiritual truth may change, even though the truth itself does not. For example, the Bible unquestionably teaches modesty in dress and general personal appearance. In the 1800's, because of styles and social attitudes, scriptural modesty undoubtedly required that ladies wear their skirts long enough to reach the ground. Anything less would have appeared immodest, therefore not very Christian. Present-day modesty does not require quite the same thing. The principle of modesty is permanent; its application is in some respects subject to change.

It is with precisely such changes that a Sunday school teacher is necessarily involved. He must be looking not only *back* (to Scripture), but also *ahead* and *around* him, giving a living, meaningful interpretation of scriptural truths which are in themselves changeless.

A teacher should also be very sensitive to change in the areas of methods and procedures. Sunday schools themselves, dating only from 1780, are really quite a new idea when viewed in the perspective of the whole history of the Christian church. Flannelboards as a tool have been in use for relatively few years. Typewriters, duplicating machines, projectors and screens—all these have had tremendous effects upon Christian teaching just as they have upon secular teaching. A Sunday school teacher who had categorically resisted *all* change would today be losing out on some important opportunities for effective teaching.

TRADITION—HOW SACRED?

Unfortunately, many well-meaning people seem to be unable to differentiate between matters of doctrine and matters of method. They have developed a great resistance to change in both areas. They may think of the lecture method as "good" and the role-playing method as "bad"—simply because the lecture method is the older of the two. But neither old nor new is good or bad of itself.

Everyone knows there is great division between the Roman Catholics on the one hand and Protestants on the other. And to a considerable extent this division springs from a difference in view of church traditions. Catholicism reveres church tradition as much as it reveres Scripture, and sometimes more. Protestantism holds that there is nothing especially binding about tradition unless it is based on the Bible.

Tradition is the pattern of established custom. Countries have traditions, and so do churches and individual families. There is nothing wrong with them as such. And human beings often enjoy the feeling of carrying on an activity which was performed by some similarly minded person or persons in a similar way many years ago. Besides lending dignity, tradition may also give stability and continuity to the group that observes it. But to have no better reason for doing something than that "it has always been done this way" is a poor condition for any teacher.

JESUS AND THE PAST

How did Jesus view tradition? He was definitely a conservative in the sense of respecting all that was best in the heritage of His people. But He *did* differentiate between the best and the rest. He picked out and called to attention "the first and great commandment" (Matthew 22:38). He literally sanctioned the breaking of Mosaic law—at least in the eyes of observers—as when His disciples plucked corn on the Sabbath (Matthew 12:1) and when He declined to stone a fallen woman (John 8:7).

Yet Jesus had enormous respect for the Old Testament Scriptures, indicated by the extent to which He quoted them. He repeatedly used such expressions as "It is written . . . ," "Did ye never read . . . ?" "Have ye not read . . . ?" "Is it not written . . . ?" "Ye have heard that it was said. . . ."

Still, despite Jesus' great respect for the past, He very clearly went against much of tradition. Time after time during His sermon on the mount (Matthew 5) He would contrast a quotation from the Hebrew past with His own "But I say unto you. . . ." It is as if He was deliberately pointing out that tradition does not have the last word on morality or righteousness.

CHANGES OF STANDARD

Many people today, Christian and otherwise, would be only too glad to reject the authority of all tradition. But notice that in every case where Jesus viewed past practice as insufficient, His own personal prescription was *always on an even higher level*. It was not that the standards of the past were too demanding; He felt that they sometimes were not demanding enough. They failed to get at the heart of many issues.

A further distinction may be helpful. The items of tradition of which Jesus was most critical were the mechanical observances that did not necessarily mean a real heart obedience on the part of the people. He did not feel bound by the strict rules of the Sabbath, nor by the ceremonial washings. But on matters of the inner heart of man, He never once ignored the standards of the earlier law by substituting some pattern that would be easier to follow.

TWO THREATS TO THE TEACHER

This question of a teacher's attitude toward the old versus the new is one of the more difficult issues he faces. Misjudgment on a teacher's part can seriously undermine his teaching effectiveness on one or both of two great rocks that threaten his course. One is *mediocrity*. A teacher who is willing to accept all the old cliches, all the "standard procedures," all the routine forms of thought and action, will soon be bogged down—and very likely boring to listen to.

On the other hand, a teacher who indulges in too much innovation is certain to draw the fire of *criticism*—both by the members of his class and by other teachers. Of course almost any teacher is going to get some criticism. But the heaviest barrage always comes against those who are trying something new and different. There are always some people who equate tradition with spirituality, and if they see you breaking traditions, they may feel that you are unspiritual, or even a heretic.

Criticism probably does as much as anything else to injure the morale of a Sunday school teacher. He must on the one hand not be so sensitive as to allow a word of disapproval to upset his teaching. But on the other hand he must not be so insensitive as to ignore what might become harmful resentment in his class. This subject is dealt with more fully in chapter 4.

WAYS OF KEEPING UP

Now, how can a Sunday school teacher keep abreast of new developments and new tools in teaching? The rules will vary according to his opportunities, but here are four things almost any teacher can do to keep from getting stale:

1. *Attend every workers meeting possible.* Pastors, Sunday school superintendents, and others are anxious to help improve the effectiveness of each teacher. Meetings for this purpose are one of the most valuable sources of new ideas and fresh approaches.

2. *Ask questions of other teachers whose opinions you respect.* The problem you face in your class may well be one that other people have faced. Their experience in dealing with it may save you many a worry and heartache.

3. *Read widely with improved teaching in mind.* Don't depend on your teacher's quarterly entirely. Range into as many areas of related reading as you can. You may be helped by reading the quarterly material of other age levels than the one you teach.

4. *Use publications which are specifically designed to help you.* For example, the *Sunday School Counselor* is a magazine specially intended for Sunday school teachers. For departmental superintendents and those who are in charge of opening assemblies, the *Superintendent's Planner* is a great help. You can also take advantage of such books as the annual *Adult Teacher's Supplement.*[1] It is the actual *use* of such aids, not their mere *existence,* which will make for better teaching and better Sunday schools.

------

[1] The items referred to are produced by the publishers of this book.

THE TRAP OF TRADITION

A certain variety of caterpillar forages for food in a single file, each caterpillar with his head in firm contact with the tail of the one in front of him. They proceed in this fashion until the leader has located a feeding area. One day a naturalist placed a line of processionary caterpillars, as they are called, on the rim of a flowerpot, and succeeded in getting the head of the leader connected with the tail of the one at the end of the line. The caterpillars then formed an unbroken circle around the rim of the flower pot. They proceeded to march without stopping for many hours. Each of the creatures apparently was depending upon the one in front of him to lead the way to food. They kept on till they dropped from fatigue.

What was their trouble? In one sense, it was a blind acceptance of what had always been the accepted way of doing things. It was an utter dependence upon tradition, habit, "standard procedure." And in this case such a guiding principle was completely insufficient. Do you know any people-sized processionary caterpillars?

QUESTIONS

1. Explain the meanings of the words, "revolutionary," "progressive," "conservative," and "reactionary."

2. Describe the primitive and civilized viewpoints as to the nature of education.

3. From nature, give examples of the principle of change and the principle of changelessness.

4. Explain why conservatism is even more sensible for a Sunday school teacher than for a public school teacher.

5. What is the difference between the Roman Catholic and Protestant views of tradition?

6. What attitude of a teacher toward tradition is most likely to stir up criticism?

7. Describe a properly balanced attitude toward criticism.

—3—

THE ONE OR THE MANY?

It has been said of the great preacher George Truett that he was "great when he preached from his pulpit, greater when he spoke . . . from the capitol steps in Washington, greater still when he addressed the Baptist World Alliance in Atlanta, but greatest of all when he stood in a country cemetery and comforted a little girl who had lost her mother."[1]

REACHING THE ONE

Most of us have long recognized that a pastor's effectiveness in dealing with the needs of a single individual is at least as important as his effectiveness when addressing a large congregation. In fact, some of the finest congregations in America have been built by men not noted for their preaching but who had the knack, the compassion, the patience, the love to deal with individual persons and their needs.

A group of university students was discussing a minister all of them admired. They began to analyze what made them like him so much. Finally one of them summed up the feelings of all. "When you talk to that man," the student said, "he listens as if what you are saying is really *important* to him!" Many of us are fortunate enough to know such people. And we invariably like them. A person who genuinely cares about other individuals—that person is universally needed and accepted.

---

[1] J. M. Price, *Jesus the Teacher*, p. 51.

The principle applies not just to pastors, but to teachers as well. When you are a Sunday school teacher, you have a relationship to your pupils which is in some points comparable to a pastoral relationship. You feel a sense of responsibility; you are looked up to for leadership; you occupy the position of a personal counselor. For these reasons it is vitally important that you be moved by a loving concern for individuals.

PEOPLE UNCLASSIFIED

It is said of Jesus, "When he saw the multitudes, he was moved with compassion" (Matthew 9:36). What moved Him? The sheer quantity of people? The mere mass of their needs? No, indeed. It is almost impossible to feel genuine compassion for a *mass* of people. The condition of a multitude may be appalling, but there is a statistical coldness about it as long as it remains a multitude.

What stirred compassion in the heart of Jesus was His continuous recognition of the plight of the individuals who made up the multitude. He saw each case in all its poignancy, its basic tragedy. Fundamentally, Jesus did not see people as belonging to great classified groups. To Him, the centurion was not merely an officer of a foreign army that was oppressing His homeland, but an individual with an individual need. And his faith was rewarded accordingly (Matthew 8:5-13).

The Lord saw Nicodemus not as a member of the sect of the Pharisees, but as a unique and needy person, possibly timid, who ought to be transformed by a new birth experience (John 3:25-36). The oft-cited instances of the Samaritan woman and the rich young ruler are other examples of Christ's deep concern for individuals. It is noteworthy that the only cases where Jesus ever avoided anyone were cases involving crowds (Matthew 5:1; 8:18; 14:22; Luke 5:15, 16, for instance). There is no instance of His ever having avoided an individual who sought Him. Over and over He stressed the personal touch.

Are crowds then not important? Of course they are. Keep in mind the compassion that moved the heart of Jesus when He saw the multitudes. But just remember that the importance of the multitude derives from the importance of the individuals who make it up.

TREND TOWARD COLLECTIVISM

This principle is easily overlooked in our time. The great processes and events of the Christian religion are all expressed in terms that apply meaningfully only to the individual—such concepts as faith, birth, adoption, baptism, prayer, study, hope, love. Basically, none of these things ever happens to a group. They are all references to what takes place in the life of the individual.

Yet, as civilization has become more and more organized, there is less and less emphasis upon the individual. The power of man's cooperative efforts is very great, and innumerable things are done today that could not possibly be accomplished by an individual alone. The unconscious result is a gradual decrease in the sense of the worth of the individual.

This trend has reached its most extreme form in communism, which teaches that the individual actually derives his worth entirely from the group or society of which he is a part. Except for society and his contribution to it, he has no real value. This philosophy has provided the excuse for denying millions

of people their personal freedom, for personal freedom
is looked upon not as a right of the individual, but
a condition granted only if it is to the advantage of
the system.

In effect, of course, the judgment of what is good
for the society rests in the hands of a few people
who actually end up with great personal power. But
communism still preaches around the world its doctrine that the individual does not really count.

BIBLE EMPHASIZES THE INDIVIDUAL

The collectivist view is diametrically opposed to
the position of the Bible and the example of the
ministry of Christ. Nevertheless, it has slowly gained
a degree of acceptance until some people even see
the Scriptures in terms of large groups, rather than
individual human beings. Many modern Jews believe
that the prophecies concerning the Messiah actually
refer to the entire nation of Israel, not to an individual Messiah at all. And, even more tragic, many
churches that consider themselves Christian have
begun to talk in terms of "the redemption of society"
rather than the redemption of the individual. In
one denomination recently, 300 ministers of a minority
racial group stated the belief that their church
". . . should place less effort on winning converts and
more on identifying itself with the entire spectrum
of a community's needs—social, economic, political,
and spiritual. Our criterion for success should not
be how many people we get to come to church, but how
successful we are in mobilizing political and other
power to work for the benefit of the entire community."

What they are advocating is the use of the church

as a tool to accomplish goals that are far from the center of the gospel. This kind of viewpoint is precisely what is wrong with a great many churches today. Surely if Jesus had given His time and attention only to political and social matters, His teachings would have been no more lasting than those of hundreds of political and social theorists. But Jesus held Himself to the real issue: the spiritual condition of the individual —and His teachings have moved the world for twenty centuries.

THE VALUE OF A MAN

In contrast to the world trend toward socialization, the Christian scheme of values puts the human individual at the top as far as earth is concerned. It was the individual "whosoever" (John 3:16) for whom God in Christ made the ultimate sacrifice. The divine plan was not to ransom a class, country, occupation, race, or any other category that lumps people together. The story of the one lost sheep (Luke 15:3-7) is a graphic example of Jesus' attitude toward salvation and the individual. A shepherd who thought chiefly in "group" terms would have behaved much differently. One cannot avoid the impression that it is the *one,* if he is lost, who counts most. Any group is of value only as the individuals who comprise it give it value.

IS SOCIALISM CHRISTIAN?

It should be pointed out that these statements do not mean Christianity is *completely* incompatible with socialism. For socialism, as a political form, may sometimes actually place great value upon the individual —albeit in the name of society. For example, the

Scandinavian countries of Europe, though in some ways among the most socialistic, also have some of the largest Christian populations, proportionately. It is wrong to equate Christianity with some one or other particular political system. Christianity is not concerned with political systems, but with individuals whom God loves and wants to save.

A SOCIAL GOSPEL?

In the era when theological liberalism was making great strides in denominations that had formerly been thoroughly conservative, the term "social gospel" came into wide use. In part it meant a gospel aimed at society rather than the individual—and thereby it became something else than the real gospel of Christ. But in part the "social gospel" meant that the most meaningful way to serve God is to serve one's fellow-men—an idea which contains a great deal of truth.

For, once one recognizes the foundational importance of the individual, the gospel unquestionably has tremendous implications for the group relationships of individuals. As with many doctrines, the doctrine of individualism can be exaggerated until it becomes a false position. If in the mind of each believer the gospel has meaning only for himself, then his Christianity can become a very narrow and selfish thing. Perhaps the most conspicuous example of this kind of thinking was the medieval attitude of exaggerated concern for personal holiness *out of all contact with the world.* This concern—to the neglect of concern for a lost world—gave Christian history its blackest hour: the Dark Ages, when monastics withdrew instead of witnessing. They had strong feelings as to what Christianity should mean within the individual, but did not see clearly what it required of the Christian in relationship to the world around him.

So by Christian individualism we do not mean an utter isolationism. Concern for the individual does not exempt any one person from responsibilities far beyond himself. Each man is still his brother's keeper.

BALANCE NEEDED

The one or the many? To maintain a scriptural, nonextreme position on this question should be a real concern of every Sunday school teacher. In the conduct of his class, his attitudes on the subject will greatly affect every aspect of his teaching. If he aims his teaching at the group as a whole, he will limit himself to the common denominators of the members of his class. If he thinks of his pupils as separate, unique individuals, he is more likely to prepare lessons that contain special morsels for this one and that one in the class.

There are, of course, many ways the differences among your class members can be described. There are differences in intelligence, in education, in motivation, in spiritual condition, and in many other qualities.

Let us think for a minute about a veriable characteristic we might call "activeness." By this we simply mean the degree to which the members of the class tend by personality to be active or passive. If we use a possible rating scale of one to ten, you may have some people in class at the two level, others at the nine level, and many in between. Now imagine that your basic mental image as you prepare for a session is of the class as a whole, as a group. You will naturally plan the period in such a way as to appeal to an activity level of about five or six—because that is the average. You will find a way to use class action, but not too much.

If on the other hand you think of your class in terms of the individualism of its members, you will plan your presentation so as to provide *some* appeal at a level as low as two *and* other appeal at a level as high as nine. This is probably the better idea, for a teacher who tries only to interest the *average* pupil will miss the many who are not average. This sample of the "balance problem" is mentioned here only as an example of the kind of difference it makes whether you think of yourself as teaching a group or as teaching individuals.

JESUS AND SOCIAL ACTION

If we agree that Jesus placed more emphasis upon the individual than the group, we can then understand why He was comparatively silent on social and political issues of His time, but outspoken on individual issues. He viewed social issues as an outgrowth of the heart condition of individuals. And Jesus believed in treating the basic problem, not the symptoms.

Many people today are interested in the question of whether or not a Christian should participate in demonstrations or other social action. Some feel it is utterly wrong; others feel that it is one's Christian duty to take an active part in social issues. Jesus' aim seems to have been to spend His time teaching what would do the most good.

If Jesus were in the shoes of a modern Christian and were considering demonstrating about something, it seems likely that He would try to find a way to demonstrate against the sin principle in individuals, rather than against the social consequences. When it comes to a Christian's participation in civic affairs, politics, all kinds of social action, the issue is: "Is this the way I can best apply the power of the gospel to human needs?" On this basis it will often become clear that the Christian çan find a more thoroughly Christlike way of expressing himself than by merely joining the expressions of others.

SELFISH INDIVIDUALISM

Sometimes those who emphasize the importance of the individual over the group are accused of fostering selfishness. It is argued that one should be willing to surrender this individuality, to become blended, submerged in the common interests of others. But again, this view does not seem to mesh very well with the teachings of our Lord. For His disciples He chose individuals from many walks of life. He did not commission a club or a clan, and He never does.

Throughout Scripture it is rather hard to find instances in which God made major use of groups or organizations. There are exceptions, such as the special tasks given to the Israelites. But generally He used anointed individuals. Sometimes they worked in close cooperation with one another, sometimes alone, but they responded as individuals nonetheless.

The most any man can give is himself. And that self has its very own set of strengths, weaknesses, peculiarities. Each man, then, has the power to give to a cause something which he alone can give, for no other has his particular combination of characteristics. Perhaps this is why the God of the Bible has put such emphasis upon the individual. If a person suppresses those very things that make his personality unique, if he blurs and dilutes those distinctions which mark him as different from all others, then in a sense he has marred the only gift it is truly in his power to give. So it is not selfish for one to maintain his individualism, except when he attempts to deny others their own.

Jesus was always superbly Himself. He imitated no one, pretended for no one. He was unique, forthright, outspoken, yet with all His power of self-expression He was never selfish. He used self as a means of service, not as an end to be served.

PERSONAL FREEDOM

Jesus' parable of the laborers (Matthew 20) is perhaps the passage which may make us most uncomfortable when we compare Jesus' philosophy with modern collectivism. But the story is simplicity itself. Jesus obviously defended the position of an employer who made separate agreements with various laborers and who ended up paying hourly rates which varied in the extreme. It's an uncomfortable parable, but there it is. It is not antiunion; it is not anticollective bargaining. But its clear emphasis is on freedom of initiative and individual choice—within the limits of honestly sticking by prior agreement.

KNOW THE PERSON

If the teacher is successfully to teach individuals, he must strive to *know* individuals. No one "knows" a group—only the individuals in it, and no two of them to the same extent. Just as a tailor must get pretty close to his customer in order to measure him for a suit of clothes, so a teacher must approach the lives of his pupils closely if he is to fit them with the truth they need. If this closeness cannot be

Proverbs 14 – 16 A wise
man feareth, and departeth
from evil but the fool
rageth and is Confident

I   Know right from
         wrong.

II   Don't be a fool.

III   fear God and have life
         everlasting.

Work out your own Salvation
with fear & trembling

DO IT NOW

Philippians 2:12

do not depend on others
to work out your Salvation
for you

2. fear God and he
will lead you in the
right for the fear of
God is your strength,

Luke 1:50 And his
mercy is on them that fear him
from Generation to Generation

achieved in the classroom, the teacher must find other means. As closely as he can, he must follow Christ's teaching example by sharing life itself with his pupils.

QUESTIONS

1. How is the position of Sunday school teacher comparable at times with that of pastor?

2. Which did Jesus often avoid, crowds or individuals?

3. Give some examples of Christian concepts that apply particularly to the individual, but hardly to groups of people.

4. Does a group derive its importance from individuals, or an individual derive his importance from the group?

5. Is socialism Christian, anti-Christian, or not particularly related to Christianity?

6. What was wrong about the medieval emphasis on monasticism?

7. Differentiate between individualism and isolationism.

8. Is it better for a teacher to aim his appeal so as to have some part of it adapted to each class member, or simply to aim it at the average class member?

9. Explain the statement, "If a person suppresses those very things that make his personality unique . . . he has marred the only gift it is truly in his power to give."

10. Explain "no one 'knows' a group."

—4—

WHAT THEY WANT OR WHAT THEY NEED?

Dr. Frank Laubach, for years the world's foremost personality in the field of adult literacy, stands teaching a group of primitive tribesmen gathered beneath a tree. He points to the letters on a simple chart displayed on an easel beside him.

"Now say after me . . . 'Ba,' " and he looks at his pupils with smiling expectation.

"Ba," they echo in earnest concentration.

"Wonderful!" Dr. Laubach exclaims. "You are learning very well. Your progress is excellent. I am sure you will be able to learn to read very quickly!"

MAKE GOALS ACHIEVABLE

In a civilized classroom Dr. Laubach's remarks might seem childish. But he knows his pupils. He knows that the greatest obstacle when an adult primitive tries to learn to read is the fear that it will turn out to be impossible for him to do so. What these pupils need most of all is confidence. So at first Dr. Laubach concentrates not so much upon the lessons as upon giving the pupils what they need—confidence. He is careful never to require of them anything that is beyond their actual abilities. He never asks them a question they cannot successfully answer. He never calls for any information until he is *sure* they know it. And he praises his pupils lavishly for every success.

42

The results? Dr. Frank Laubach has taught more adults to read than perhaps any man in human history. His method and his influence have reached out to millions more he has never seen himself. The method he has made famous has much behind it—both spiritually and scientifically. But one of the basic ingredients is the *setting of achievable goals.*

Most of us are not engaged in teaching primitive savages in some remote corner of the earth. But yet we can profit from Dr. Laubach's simple principle—the principle of setting goals which are actually achievable—then leading our students to the victorious accomplishment of those goals.

We might as well face it, the pupils in our classes are not likely to be perfect, *ever.* We want to free their lives from sin and misery. We want to lead them to a knowledge of God and the Bible. We want to make them strong, functioning members of the Body of Christ. We want to lead them up the road toward perfection just as far as we can possibly manage to do. But our success in these attempts will depend very much upon our willingness to set lowly, step-by-step, practicable goals our students can understand and accept.

AVOID EXTREMES

If you have been a Christian for as much as a few years, it is a safe guess that you have already had, somewhere or other, an opportunity to observe one or both of the following kinds of Christian leadership:

1. *The popular personality.* This person makes a success of Christian service largely by the force of his individual charm and his ability to make a presentation which is popular to his hearers. In his most extreme characterization he will dilute or even aban-

don Christian principle in order to attract listeners either to himself or to his message.

2. *The super-spiritual saint.* This individual may "hew to the line" so rigorously that his listeners feel browbeaten, discouraged, and somewhat hopeless. Who can ever satisfy his standards of perfection? In his most extreme characterization, this kind of leader seems to be living in the clouds, completely out of touch with reality. And often he ends up speaking mostly to empty seats.

There is no law that says a teacher must fall into one or the other of these traps. Most of the Christian leaders you know and respect probably live somewhere between these two extremes. But the extremes serve to call attention to the dual temptation that comes sooner or later to any Christian teacher. On the one hand, you may be tempted to give up everything else in order to make your pupils responsive and enthusiastic to what you are doing and saying. On the other hand, you may have your eyes glued so firmly on the shining truth that you fail to make it seem real and achievable to your listeners. Week by week, lesson by lesson, every teacher needs careful balance in this important area.

EVALUATE PUPILS' MATURITY

In any drugstore you can see displays of tablets and capsules marked "children's." There are vitamin pills—and *children's* vitamin pills. There are aspirin tablets—and *children's* aspirin tablets. There are laxatives—and *children's* laxatives. What is the difference from the regular? Aside from adjustment in the size of the dosage, the difference is that the children's products are simply made to taste better.

They are chewable; they are chocolate flavored; they are sweet; or they are at least smaller to make them more easily swallowed.

There is an important principle here. Adults presumably understand their needs well enough to be willing to take the medicines they should have—even if those medicines do not taste very good. The need itself is enough to motivate an adult. But children do not understand their needs very well. And all too often they do not have a strong enough sense of need to make them willing to take a medicine that has an unpleasant taste. Unless the experience of taking it is pleasant *in itself*, they are not interested.

It is a rather threadbare pun to call the gospel a "gos-pill." However, there is a sense in which thinking of it this way can help you as a teacher to understand a special problem you have. How much sugar coating must you give the truth to make it acceptable to your class? How much will they receive—and act upon— just because they need it? How broken up, diluted, or sweetened must you make the truth in order to get them to accept it?

This is a question which faces not only the Sunday school teacher. Anyone in a position of religious leadership has the same problem to contend with. The pastor asks himself, "Should I preach on the subject which will be enthusiastically received—or on the subject which is most needed, even if the people will not receive it willingly?" The youth leader says to himself, "Is it better to get 30 young people to attend a social, or to get only three or four to attend a prayer meeting?" A men's leader asks, "Which is better: a large group at a breakfast session or a small group at a work session?"

It all boils down to, "How much should we sugar-coat the pill?"

BALANCE IS POSSIBLE

Of course orthodox doctrine does not necessarily mean colorless presentation. Most of us have seen and heard Christian speakers who have managed to make the most demanding challenge for sacrifice, yet state it in terms that have strong appeal. And this is the ideal. But the necessary process of self-evaluation requires that each teacher consider for himself whether he is sometimes committing an error in one direction or the other. The one who says, "The important thing is attention—spiritual details will come later," is sometimes covering up the fact that he is simply captivating his listeners, but not Christianizing them. And the teacher who says, "My pupils just have no hunger for God's Word—that's why they stay away," is often only making an excuse for his failure to stimulate spiritual appetite.

How much did Jesus adapt His presentation of the truth to the desires and interests of His listeners? Did He simply state the truth and "let the chips fall where they may"? Or did He withhold the truth—except those parts for which He felt His listeners were ready?

Perhaps the classic story which does most to give us the answer to this question is that of the rich young ruler who came to Jesus and asked, "What good thing shall I do, that I may have eternal life?" (Matthew 19:16). Here was a man who was already highly motivated when he came to Jesus. One of the gospel accounts tells us that he was so interested that he actually came *running* to ask for Jesus' advice (Mark

10:17) . Yet he shows us one of the clearest examples of a case in which Jesus did *not* succeed in what He must have intended or hoped to do. For the story ends up with the rich young ruler departing sorrowfully. There is no hint that he ever yielded his will and did what Jesus asked him to do—sell his possessions and give the income to the poor. At first glance it might seem that Jesus simply laid out in cold, idealistic terms a difficult prescription, quite regardless of whether or not the young man was likely to accept it. He seems almost to have taken a "take it or leave it" kind of attitude.

But a closer examination of the story will show this was not actually Jesus' approach. The following factors are worth noting in this teaching situation:

1. In this instance, Jesus did not volunteer His advice—He was asked. Throughout our Lord's ministry it is noticeable that He had a quite different approach to people who asked Him specific questions, as compared with His approach to those who had so far asked nothing. Some of His strongest scorn seems to have been reserved for those who came to Him with questions they thought might trap Him. For example, the scribes and Pharisees brought to Him the woman that had been caught in adultery, asking Him, "But what sayest thou?" (John 8:5) . His ensuing actions drove them away just as effectively as did His attack upon the moneychangers in the temple.

2. Jesus began by identifying carefully the rich young ruler's stage of spiritual development. Just as at the drugstore the amount of artificial flavoring or sugar coating necessary on a medication depends on the stage of maturity of the consumer, so Jesus recognized that the truth can be stated much more

bluntly to one who by experience should be well prepared for it. The rich young ruler had a background which should have prepared him well for the high ideal Jesus was to set for him. The fact that his response is deficient does not mean that Jesus' approach was at fault. We can safely say, based upon the many other stories in the gospels, that Jesus would have been much more mild and gentle in His approach if the rich young ruler had been a person with less background in the truth.

This is another way of saying that the more light a pupil has, the more direct and concentrated can be the "medicine" prescribed.

GRADE YOUR ADAPTATION

In recent years there has been an ever-increasing emphasis upon the importance of carefully grading our Sunday school lessons. More and more research has tended to show that the differences between the viewpoints of different age groups are important—even when the ages may be only a year or two apart. The recognition of these differences has produced refinement in the choice of subject materials and in the methods used to present them.

But perhaps the most significant importance of grading is in this area of making the truth acceptable. Generally speaking, the younger the age group, the more the teacher must couch the truth in terms which make it interesting and acceptable to the pupil. Keep the drugstore in mind. The vitamins, no matter how important and nutritious, must be made to taste good if the young are to accept them.

We must also recognize that there are important differences in maturity within an individual class. Not all juniors are equally mature in thinking, nor in spiritual experience; not all high schoolers are equally prepared for more adult truth. One of a teacher's biggest problems is to evaluate the necessary balance he must use between what his pupils *want* and what they *need*.

All this leads directly to the question of pupil motivation. The word *motivation* means that which causes movement. It refers to the moving force that causes the pupil to act, to learn. People, no matter what their age, do not learn easily unless they want to learn. Creating the "want to" is often the biggest part of the teacher's job.

In a way, the problem of motivating pupils remains enormous no matter what age level you teach. Perhaps at the earlier age levels a greater amount of teacher stimulus is required for the learning of a specific lesson or thought. However, the teacher at the younger age level has the advantage of having nature on his side: the pupil's whole life is oriented around the learning process.

At older age levels, a teacher may not have to do as much to stimulate student interest in a particular subject. The pupil's own background may provide sufficient motivation for his interest. Yet the teacher of the older age levels faces the increasing problem of motivating pupils to learn *at all.* Many a teacher of adults has reached near despair as he realizes that so many of his class members feel they have already arrived at a knowledge of the truth. Some of them feel that they simply tolerate a teacher's comments, but have nothing to learn, really, from what is said in the class.

The fact is, of course, that each age level has its

own special problems. And for each the problem of motivation looms large on the teacher's list of obstacles that must be coped with.

UNDERSTAND MOTIVATION

Educators identify two basic kinds of motivation. If we consider motivation as being the basic "reason" why a pupil does something, the following distinction can be made. One kind of motivation is based upon getting the pupil to do the thing because he sees the inherent value in doing it. That is, he understands why it is important, what he will get out of it, how it relates to himself and the kingdom of God. This kind of motivation we call *intrinsic*. It simply means that the reason is built into the thing itself. The other kind of motivation called *extrinsic,* is a matter of getting a pupil to do the right thing because he has been given some extra or outside reason for doing it. He is led to do the right thing, but not necessarily for the right reason.

Example: When you increase your class attendance because the subject matter and the way it is handled fascinates pupils to such an extent that they do not want to miss one of the sessions—that is intrinsic motivation. If you increase class attendance by offering a free dinner, a gift, or some form of public recognition—this is extrinsic motivation.

Example: If a pupil memorizes a Scripture verse because he understands the importance of the verse to himself and to his Christian service, this is intrinsic motivation. If he memorizes a verse simply because he wants to save face—avoid appearing ignorant or uncooperative, or avoid embarrassing himself in front of his girl friend—this is extrinsic motivation.

The two motivations are not always clear-cut; they may sometimes blend into one another. And it is not accurate to say that intrinsic motivation is always right and extrinsic motivation is always wrong. Circumstances alter cases.

In general, the more mature a group of pupils, the more appeal can be made to intrinsic motivation. To take a secular example, a young school child cannot be motivated to memorize his multiplication tables because he understands how valuable they will be to him later on. He must generally be given some extrinsic motivation—by way of his grade card, his teacher's commendation, or his standing among his fellow students—in order to learn. However, by the time a college student reaches graduate school, he *should* be motivated more by a desire to know and understand the material he is studying, less by a desire simply to please his teacher, his family, or his fellow students.

This principle also applies in Sunday school. To the more mature student, a teacher can make an appeal based upon an understanding of the subject and a desire to increase that understanding. To the less mature student, a teacher may have to resort to the introduction of other, more extrinsic motivations in order to get the pupil to learn.

Educators in general believe that intrinsic motivation is by far the more desirable—when it is practicable. But never forget for a moment that extrinsic motivation is better than none at all. The Sunday school youngster who comes to class because he "likes the teacher" or "enjoys the atmosphere" is probably better off than the one who does not come at all. And it often happens that pupils who participate in a Sunday school class for purely extrinsic reasons to begin with may later on attend because of a truly mature understanding of the benefits and values of the study material being taught.

At most age levels, a teacher will have to recognize that a blend of both kinds of motivation is necessary.

USE THREE APPROACHES

Every learner is motivated by:

1. His intellect (his power to think),
2. His emotions (his power to feel), and
3. His will (his power to choose).

Jesus was careful to appeal to all three parts of the human personality. In His parable of the talents (Matthew 25), it is noticeable that He appeals to His listeners' reasoning power. He gives them a logical sense of proportion as He describes what was expected of the servants who were entrusted with five talents, two talents, and one talent. He also appeals to His listeners' emotions as He portrays the feelings experienced by the master of the vineyard and by the servants he left behind (for example, the fear of the man who was given only one talent). And He appeals to His listeners' sense of volition (will) as He makes it plain that the fate of each servant was determined clearly by his own freedom of choice as to what he would do with the portion entrusted to him.

Think back over the most effective sermons you have ever heard. You will probably find that such sermons have contained a clear appeal to intellect, to emotion, and to human will. These are three vital parts of human personality. Any attempt to influence human personality must inevitably deal with these factors. Christ's teaching did. To be effective as a Christian teacher, you must also.

Perhaps it is worthwhile to conclude our consideration of this subject by pointing out that, no matter how important a truth, it is not going to accomplish its purpose unless it is accepted. And it is the teacher's job to get it accepted. The reason that mid-twentieth century Sunday schools lose such a large proportion of their teen-agers is that our schools have all too often failed to give these young people intrinsic motivations which are valid to them. As Christian adults we may be perfectly aware that there are overpoweringly important reasons why teen-agers should attend church, should pray, should read the Bible, and should live a Christian life in general. But teen-agers, passing as they are from childish dependence to adult independence, are not prepared to base their actions upon secondhand motivation. They must have their own reasons—reasons which are *to them* important and sufficient—or they will not act. Part of our task is to motivate them, to give them reasons which are important enough to *them*.

QUANTITY OR QUALITY

There is a basic theological question at issue here. It is a question which is faced not only by your Sunday school class, but by your whole church and entire fellowship. Should we try to reach a great many people with only a small fraction of the truth? Or should we concentrate on reaching a small number of people with a more complete revelation of the truth? You will find that pastors and other Christian workers in our church—and other churches—are divided on this issue. Some emphasize a purely evangelistic ministry, striving to get "decisions for Christ," but doing little to lead people into the deeper truths of the gospel. Others are perennially concerned about strengthening and deepening the saints; they emphasize a profound and sometimes complex comprehension of Scripture, and have very little time for immature Christians whose discipleship seems to be on a superficial level.

You must decide for yourself: Is either extreme necessary? What can I do to motivate both kinds of people? How can I give my class the teaching it *needs,* and yet make my teaching be what the class *wants* to a reasonable degree?

In condensed form, it seems possible to state Christ's guiding principle in this way: A teacher should go to all possible lengths to adapt to the *understanding* of his listeners; but he is *not* obligated to adapt his message to the *moral values* of his listeners. Time and again Jesus adapted His message to those who heard Him by using those idioms and forms of speech that would make the truth easily comprehensible to them. By the seaside He talked about being "fishers of men." In the fields, He talked about "harvest." On the hillsides He referred to Himself as "the good shepherd." But never once did He change His message in order to meet the warped or crippled moral viewpoints of those to whom He spoke. In matters of right and wrong He was always unequivocal.

Bible truth, presented to people, always forces them to decide on issues of personal behavior. The teacher's function is not to make the decisions *easier,* but to make them *clearer,* more vivid, more completely understood.

QUESTIONS

1. State the two opposite extremes in the matter of making the gospel attractive.

2. Why did Jesus set such a high standard for the "rich young ruler"?

3. What is the meaning of "motivation"?

4. Why is motivation for learning often easier to produce in younger pupils than in older?

5. What is the difference between intrinsic motivation and extrinsic motivation?

6. Which is the more desirable kind of motivation?

7. What are the three parts of human personality to which motivational appeals may be made?

8. To which should a teacher be most willing to adapt: to the pupil's understanding, or to the pupil's moral standards?

9. What is meant by the statement, "The teacher's function is not to make the (pupil's) decisions *easier,* but to make them *clearer . . .*"?

10. Among what age levels is extrinsic motivation most called for?

—5—

TELL THEM OR SHOW THEM?

A certain church needed to raise money for a building program. The deacon board decided to call in the services of a professional fund-raising organization. One of the first steps was to have the organization's representative meet with the deacons. At his first opportunity to speak, the fund-raiser looked carefully around at every man in the room. "Gentlemen," he said, "my organization can work no miracles. And I may as well tell you right from the beginning that our plan depends on this principle: Every man on this board must be willing to make public the amount of his own contribution to the building fund!"

This viewpoint is a little startling to us. Some of us may resent the fact that even so much as the church treasurer has to know how much we give in a year! We would think it highly improper for the public in general to know the details of our giving to the church. And, happily, most of our churches allow us the privacy we want in this respect. But the professional fund-raising agency has put its finger on an important principle: If you are going to lead other people, you must do so not only by what you say—you must follow through by doing what you are asking others to do. The power of example is an old but undiminished power. And example, to be effective, must be *visible*.

POWER AND PROBLEMS

For a teacher, this principle has special importance —and special problems. In teachers meetings or workers training sessions it is common for us to make noble allusions to the power of example. But are we being realistic? In the extremely limited time of our Sunday school session—approximately one hour per week—is it actually possible for a teacher to demonstrate scriptural truth by his own life?

The fact is that on many basic issues of living, we have kept our lives just about as private as we prefer to keep our financial affairs. For the most part, our pupils never see us except under dress-up conditions when we are on our best behavior. They neither see nor hear us as we practice our own private devotions. They are unable to observe how we cope— or fail to cope—with the exasperations of a long and trying day. They cannot look in on our family group at mealtimes to see whether we are congenial or crabby. They are not around to see how we respond to an overcharge—or to receiving too much change—in a restaurant.

In a way, it is as if circumstances have conspired to keep us from teaching our pupils in that most effective of all ways—by example. Jesus was able to teach hour by hour, day after day, in close and continuous contact with His disciples. He was not limited by the walls of a classroom nor by the ringing of a bell to end a teaching period.

Yes, our circumstances are different. Are we then justified in assuming that personal example is not as important a teaching tool for us as it was for our Lord?

The answer is no. *Even the lack of example is itself*

a lesson in example. That is, if our pupils observe us "dealing with" Christianity only in the artificial atmosphere of the classroom, we are in effect teaching them that Christianity is only good for artificial, classroom situations. A teacher teaches by his whole life. There is no way around it.

SOME HIDE EXAMPLE

Of course many a Sunday school teacher has tried to isolate his teaching from the rest of his life. His Sunday school class is a nice little compartment of his total activity. He thinks of it as totally insulated from his family life, his recreational life, or how he makes his living. Sooner or later this attitude traps him, for it will inevitably lead to a certain amount of hypocrisy in the classroom.

By thinking of his teaching apart from the rest of his life, he will soon come to think that the rest of his life does not particularly matter to his teaching. And eventually his teaching will be rendered ineffective by one or the other of two possible results: either his pupils will eventually discover that his life is inconsistent with his teaching, or, if he succeeds in keeping them from finding this out, they will come to feel that a person's private life has little or nothing to do with his Christianity—because in their teacher the two are kept quite separate.

WORDS PLUS ACTION

Although in our culture it is not practicable to teach our pupils by long hours of daily contact, we must recognize that the closer we can come to this ideal, the more effective we are likely to be. Invariably, the teachers who are making the greatest impact for the kingdom of God are those who have a concern and a personal involvement with their pupils far beyond the limits of the classroom and the Sunday school hour.

Jesus highly valued both His words and His actions as instruments of teaching. He said of His words, "They are spirit, and they are life" (John 6:63). Yet He said of His actions, "Believe me for the very works' sake" (John 14:11).

Teachers, let's face the uncomfortable fact: Christian leadership implies a public life, open to scrutiny by others. The reward is that, by letting others see our lives openly, they may be touched and molded to conform to the image of Him we follow. Paul, himself a tremendously effective teacher, considered his work " . . . to make ourselves an ensample unto you to follow us" (2 Thessalonians 3:9).

LIVING IN PUBLIC

But what about the right of privacy: Cannot a Sunday school teacher reasonably expect that his pupils will leave him alone except during class time? The answer is no, although of course any teacher can condition his pupils to leave him alone in this way. But he will pay a tremendous price in loss of teaching effectiveness. For if he has succeeded in stimulating so much interest that a pupil desires contact—and therefore learning experience—outside the Sunday school class, he will stifle this success as soon as he makes it apparent that he does not welcome such a relationship.

Then how much responsibility does a teacher have for his pupils *outside* the classroom? The answer is not easy, but here it is: The teacher is responsible

for doing everything possible to influence the lives of
his pupil for good, no matter where or when.

Look at the life of Jesus, our great teaching example.
He required privacy only for meditation and prayer.
And sometimes He invited the company of His
disciples even in this sacred activity. It is noteworthy
that even in the agony of the Garden He allowed
some to be close enough to hear His words—the words
of a very private and very painful struggle. Most of
us have never thought about it, but perhaps personal
privacy was one of the greatest sacrifices Jesus made
for the sake of His teaching ministry.

We are much more likely to think about our own
sacrifice. It is not pleasant to put up with intrusions,
prying questions, thoughtless and sometimes selfish
invasions of our private lives. But what are we trying
to do, teach by word alone? If so, we must resign
ourselves to a very lowly second best as teachers.
Jesus let His followers see Him live, virtually 24
hours a day. Granted, our situation may not make
this possible, but is the *willingness* there? Here is a
vital measure of attitude in a teacher. Remember,
the closer we come to the disciple method, the more
effective we are likely to be.

Some of our foreign missionaries work in circumstances that make it more nearly possible for them to
use the disciple method fairly fully. And Dr. Eugene
Nida of the American Bible Society frankly advises
missionaries, "Never do anything alone; always have
a young Christian with you to learn from what he sees
you do." Why? Well, if a missionary takes time, say,
to pray for a sick person, the time spent has a certain
value in his ministry. But if he prays for the sick
person *in the alert and observing presence of some*

young Christian national, the time so spent has a double value: it is a ministry to the sick and it is also a living *example* of ministry to the observer. Dr. Nida recognizes that the day-by-day routine work of a missionary has enormous teaching value. And it is a shame not to take full advantage of that value.

To apply this principle to your own situation, have you ever considered inviting a member or two of your Sunday school class to go along with you in some activity (not necessarily on Sunday) which could have learning possibilities for them? A hospital visit, an overnight business trip, a financial transaction, a fishing expedition—each has its own possibilities for teaching. Use them to the utmost!

TEACHING ON THE MOVE

It would probably surprise us if we knew how much of Jesus' teaching was actually given "on the go." He walked many miles on many roads, and they were not silent miles. He used the environment—nature—as a background for many of His lessons. He talked about fields and laborers, vineyards and landowners, sheep and shepherds, vines and branches, and the lessons stuck in the minds and hearts of His disciples.

Today we do not spend much time walking through the countryside with our pupils. But does not even a modern automobile offer wonderful opportunities for conversation? (Or would we rather relax and listen to music or a ball game?) Our environment of contact may not offer the same *form,* but it certainly offers the same *function.* In place of a Galilean fish fry, we may have a modern restaurant—but does it not offer its own opportunities for meaningful communication with some potential learner?

NO SECRETS

This is the destiny of the true teacher: a life of unrelenting self-discipline, seeing each situation in terms of its teaching opportunities. And most of us have never come even faintly close to the ideal of "Never do anything alone." But Jesus, our example, came very close indeed.

Lest we feel too much like sacrificial lambs in this connection, it is well to realize that a life lived "in the open" before our pupils has benefits to ourselves as well as to them. For any human being, a secret is a strain. Any aspect of life which, for one reason or another, must be concealed from other people creates tensions that can seriously affect mental and physical health. No one lives a double life comfortably, even when the two roles are both legal. The fewer secrets you have, the happier you are likely to be.

TALKING WITHOUT BRAGGING

If and when you have accepted the teacher's responsibility to expose his life to his pupils as much as possible, another important problem remains: to what extent should a teacher call attention to his own behavior? For example, in terms of practical application, should a teacher mention to his pupils that he makes it a point to pray for ten minutes each morning before he dresses for the day? Or that he resigned his job because his boss wanted him to do something dishonest? Or that he presented a turkey to a destitute family last Thanksgiving? Or that he came to Sunday school this morning despite the fact that a long trip had deprived him of all but three hours sleep?

No teacher likes to feel that he is bragging. And

if one calls attention to his own "good behavior,"
is he not being something of a Pharisee? On the other
hand, did not Jesus teach us to let our righteous
deeds be known when he said, "Let your light so
shine before men, that they may see your good
works..."? (Matthew 5:16).

To avoid bragging on the one hand and undue
secrecy on the other is admittedly a delicate problem
for a teacher. Like the rest of the teacher's problems
it probably has no quick, easy answer. If a teacher
hides his good works, he may be guilty of hiding his
light under a bushel. If he flaunts his good works,
he is guilty of self-righteousness. Where is the proper
balance between the two?

MOTIVE A KEY

An important clue lies in the *why* of what we do.
Notice that Jesus condemns doing things to be "seen
of men" (Matthew 6:5). The point here is not *what*
is done, but *why* it is done. If you call attention
to one of your "good deeds" with the purpose of
obtaining admiration or status, your good deed goes
for naught. But if you call attention to something you
have done, aiming only to encourage others to do the
same, you are performing the legitimate function of a
teacher. Both Jesus and Paul repeatedly called attention to their own performances and encouraged others
to imitate them. This was not conceit, it was actually
an acceptance of responsibility—the deep and all-
devouring responsibility of the teacher. Is modesty
sometimes a luxury a good teacher cannot afford?

In practical terms, how will your class know the
reality of your ideal of daily personal devotions unless
you tell them about your own practice? How will

they know you *really* believe in tithing unless you assure them you practice it? Keep your motives pure, and never mind the modest niceties of social custom.

SAYING WHAT YOU THINK

Another problem in this area concerns the teacher's exposure of his personal opinion on controversial issues. Do pupils have a right to know what he thinks? Or is a teacher justified in objectively presenting both sides of an issue and ending up only with a "take your choice" offer to his pupils?

On this question it is more difficult for us to learn from Jesus' individual example. For his personal opinions were not mere personal opinions—they were the epitome of truth, the attitudes of God Himself. He spoke with authority, "not as the scribes" (Matthew 7:29). Presumably the scribes were full of equivocation and personal attitudes. Many of us may feel more like the scribes than like Jesus on this point! We are not sure; we fumble, change our minds, see both sides of an issue, feel unqualified to make a positive statement. So what should we do, act dogmatic whether we are sure or not?

No. The answer is honesty. A teacher has both the right and the responsibility to let his opinion be known—provided it is plainly labeled as his opinion. All of us teach various truths with various degrees of certainty. Some we would stake our lives on. Some we are convinced of by personal experience. Some we have read, understood, and accepted. Some make only theoretical sense. Some we see accepted by other teachers, but tend to question in our own minds. It is foolhardy to teach firm conviction and theoretical speculation with equal fervor. When you are sure, say so. When you lean one way on an issue, say so—but point out there are others who lean the other way. When you mean "probably," *say* "probably," not "positively."

HONEST ANSWERS

Some teachers pride themselves on their ability to sidestep a pupil's questions. They deliberately make their answers equivocal or vague. This may hide the teacher's ignorance—or his heretical views—but it is blatantly unfair to the pupil. An honest question deserves an honest answer. If you don't know, admit you don't know—then try to find out. If the question pulls you in two directions, explore both directions—even the one which may seem new or unconventional.

The secular educator may call this "intellectual honesty." It is an essential in all education, but most essential of all in Christian education. A Christian teacher must be honest in intellectual, emotional, and spiritual matters. Perhaps this is just another way of saying that the Christian teacher must live an exposed life. He must both state his beliefs and live them. He must commit himself, not hedge. He must say where he stands—or doesn't stand—even if it means he later has to admit being wrong.

Inter-Varsity Christian Fellowship, a great international society which strives to bring the evangelical message to university campuses throughout the world, has noticed an important characteristic of today's college students. And it is a characteristic which may surprise those who expect to find nothing but intellectual radicalism. When college students assess a Christian's testimony, they are not looking for scholarship, emotion, or traditional dignity. What they crave is *honesty*. Speak to them, and their questions afterward will probe what you really think, really know, or have really experienced. If you claim to believe something, have you really laid your life on the line for that belief? That's what they want to know. And isn't this also what the pupils of your Sunday school class want to know?

There it is: for the Christian teacher there is no place to hide. Many a brilliant lecturer has had his efforts nullified by inconsistency in his own example, or by hidden pockets in his personal life. To teach is to live, and living is a 24-hours-a-day affair.

QUESTIONS

1. What are the dangers of a teacher's isolating his teaching from the other aspects of his life?

2. What does the record of Jesus' life teach us about the privacy of a teacher?

3. Describe the idea contained in the advice, "Never do anything alone. . . ."

4. Why is an open life the happiest one?

5. Name some of the situations (besides in the Sunday school session on Sunday) in which a Sunday school teacher may help his pupils learn.

6. When is pointing to your own performance not conceit?

7. To what extent should a teacher reveal his own opinions on controversial issues?

8. Is it better for a teacher to admit his uncertainty in some matters, or to pretend a positiveness he may not feel?

—6—

PRINCIPLES OR PRACTICE?

St. Augustine is often quoted as prescribing, "in essentials—unity; in nonessentials—liberty; but in all things—charity!" This is a great truth compressed into little space. And, as a motto, it is almost completely uncontroversial. That is, it is probably accepted by every Christian who has ever heard or read it. The controversy comes when one seeks to *apply* it.

WHAT IS "ESSENTIAL"?

But where is the line between essentials and nonessentials? That question has plagued theologians for centuries. It is actually the factor which accounts for most doctrinal differences and denominational splits in the Christian church.

For example, consider the Pentecostal doctrine that speaking in tongues is one of the essential evidences of the experience of being baptized in the Holy Spirit. Our study of Scripture convinces us that tongues *is* an essential part of the Pentecostal experience. And it is actually the "essentialness" which is the doctrinal issue. Quite a few non-Pentecostal denominations are prepared to accept the fact that the baptism of the Holy Spirit *can* be accompanied by the phenomenon of speaking in tongues. The point with which they take issue is the idea that tongues is *essential*.

As another example, there are some seventh-day denominations which believe the observation of the Sabbath is absolutely essential. Most Christian denominations seriously doubt the "essentialness" of this practice.

There are relatively few beliefs or practices concerning which one group of Christians says "always," while another group of Christians insists "never." More often the one group says "always," and the other group says "not necessarily!"

All of this is simply to point out that there may be a great deal of difference between agreeing on a basic statement of principle (such as the Augustinian motto above) and agreeing on what that principle means when applied to actual personal behavior.

HOW MUCH DETAIL?

This chapter deals with the basic dilemma: How closely should a teacher apply the truth he teaches to the individual lives of his pupils?

At first it may seem obvious that the teacher should apply the truth as closely as possible. After all, the truth can have meaning only in terms of actual behavior. It is no good to tell a primary he should be "unselfish," but fail to explain to him the kind of behavior unselfishness should produce. When he is told that Jesus wants him to be unselfish, he must immediately be given concrete examples—and better yet, opportunities for personal action—which will give him some tangible association for the concept of unselfishness. (In the typical classroom situation, he can be asked to share his crayons, his workbook, or other materials with one or more other members of the class.)

MATURITY MAKES A DIFFERENCE

But the answer to our question is not quite so simple as saying, "The teacher must apply the truth as much as possible." For again the question of differences in maturity enters the picture. If a pupil grows up being told specifically at every stage of his development exactly what each Christian principle means, he will sooner or later be in serious trouble. The trouble comes about because:

1. No teacher can give all the examples and life situations to which the principle is applicable, and

2. The pupil will come to depend upon the interpretations which are handed to him rather than those he is able to think through for himself. And he will not be able to live indefinitely on "predigested" morals.

To put it another way, here is a teacher's great dilemma:

1. The *less* he "spells out" what it means to be a Christian, the easier will his pupils misunderstand Christianity, and the likelier they will be to consider it something vague and theoretical.

2. Yet, the *more* the teacher "spells out" Christianity, the easier will his pupils lapse into a shallow dependence on do's and don'ts rather than facing life's issues for themselves.

Sooner or later every person is going to face situations that have not been touched upon by his teachers, no matter how conscientious they may have been. His success at Christian living is not going to be determined merely by a kind of moral reflex action as he reacts to situations for which he has been conditioned. Rather, his success is going to depend upon his ability to apply to each life situation the deep and basic principles he has learned by his exposure to the Bible, the Lord Jesus Christ, and the Holy Spirit.

No teacher enjoys being asked uncomfortable questions. Yet the uncomfortable ones are exactly the ones which are the greatest problems to our pupils— and therefore the ones with which they are in the greatest need of help. What do you answer when a pupil asks, "Is it all right for me as a Christian to join my high school pep club?" How can you possibly give a meaningful answer unless you know a great deal about the high school, the pep club and its activities, and the attitudes of your pupil? Will his joining the club mean he has to attend every athletic event at the school? If so, how seriously will this interfere with his church life? Does the pep club have social activities that may lead him to compromise his Christian testimony? Can he be a better witness inside the club or outside it? To what extent will club activities contribute legitimately to his education? Will he feel needlessly restricted and rejected if he cannot join? All these questions enter into the answering of the first one. In fact, a wise teacher might well answer the pupil's original question by posing a few of those which follow it above.

DANGERS OF THE MECHANICAL

We all know cases where people who consider themselves highly Christian have actually fallen into a kind of mechanized Christianity. Their religion consists of the observation of a bunch of rigid do's and don'ts they have been taught. They seem morally unable to cope with problems which do not appear on their list. Someone, somewhere (and probably over an extended period of time) has conditioned them to believe that being a Christian consists of such and such and such things—and of abstaining from such and such and such things. They have learned well; they now believe firmly that these observances make up Christianity—and that's it.

Obviously, no one's list can actually include all of the things a Christian should or should not do. The Christian life consists of facing each life situation with attitudes and judgments that spring from the Christlife vibrant within. While many of these specific responses may be highly predictable, no one can possibly list them all. When we try to do so, we may create chaos for those we are trying to teach.

Take for example the question of personal holiness or sanctification. Some teachers have succeeded well at giving teen-agers a balanced, overall concept of what the holy life means. But many teachers, by limiting their teaching to a narrow list of examples, have produced a very limited view of holiness.

Some of our young people have been taught very specifically what holiness means when applied to drinking, dancing, smoking, gambling, or going to the movies. However, since dating behavior is often left off the list, there are frequent cases of Christian young people who, though abstaining from all the things mentioned above, may indulge in some very unholy behavior in a parked car after a church service.

Is it because they want to be wicked? No, not basically. The trouble is that someone has managed to teach them a few specifics without teaching them a principle strong enough to guide them when the specifics vary.

Does all this mean there is danger in too detailed an application of the truth? Yes, this is a very real danger. If Jesus taught anything, He taught that it is invisible desires which are most important, not simply visible behavior. By concentrating upon visible behavior we have sometimes de-emphasized the importance of inner attitudes and motives.

Sooner or later, many of those we teach will begin to detect seeming inconsistencies. They will feel our rules are arbitrary. They will not understand why some things are on the forbidden list and others are not. They will resent what they do not understand. Before long they will rebel at the arbitrariness of the rules. And if they have been brought up to live by the list or nothing—they may start living by nothing.

If Jesus were telling parables today, would He tell the same ones He told in the year A.D. 30? The points and purposes would be the same, but the form of the stories would certainly be different. He would speak of ranchers and businessmen, factory workers, secretaries, accountants, housewives, teachers, and preachers. He chose the well-known, everyday settings of Galilee and Judea for the stories He told His disciples. There is no reason to think He would be less adaptive if He lived and ministered in our time. He was never satisfied with the truth as an abstraction; He wanted to make it live in the hearts of the people who heard Him. To do that, He had to make it real and alive to them.

The problem very clearly is: How does a teacher instill Christian principles so deeply into the lives of his pupils that the principles will be truly understood, assimilated, and lived out in the specific details of day-by-day practice? Like many another question teachers face, this has no single, quick, push-button solution. It is concerned with the whole problem of building character—a process which is long, tedious, difficult, and not too well understood by most of us.

Teaching character is not like building a boat. Nobody can give you reliable, step-by-step instructions to follow. And if they did, the results would still not be accurately predictable.

But there it is, squarely across the path of the teacher like an enormous roadblock: "How shall I build Christian principles into the lives of my pupils?"

WHAT JESUS DID

For help, we can do no better than turn to the example of the Lord Jesus Himself. To what extent did He interpret His principles for the individual, personal lives of His disciples? Three observations may help.

1. *Jesus was not afraid to state a principle plainly.* He would say clearly, "Therefore all things whatsoever ye would that men should do to you, do ye even so to them" (Matthew 7:12). He would pronounce with the greatest possible emphasis, "Ye must be born again" (John 3:7). His language was remarkably free from words such as "probably," "more or less," "generally speaking," "usually," "but. . . ."

A statement of principle is always a risk. As a teacher, when you make such a statement you are commiting yourself to a certain position—which you may later have to defend. You may face the embarrassment of having to alter or modify your position. For these reasons there are a good many people today who would rather not state a principle at all. A high-ranking official in one denomination told reporters plainly that he did not believe in living by principles—because they tended to be too rigid. He felt that each person should just do the best he can with each life situation as he comes to it.

But principles are very important hitching posts for the human heart and mind. Many a life has been saved from shipwreck because of the memory of a principle or rule learned long ago. The young person who carries with him the words of his mother, "Never go anywhere unless you feel you can take Jesus there with you," has an instant measuring stick which is useful day after day.

No, Jesus was not afraid to state a principle. He did not try to make an eternally binding pronouncement on every subject; neither should you. But in the major areas of life, our Lord spoke words that will live forever. Don't hesitate to quote His principles. Don't hesitate to state them in modern terms. Where you can state a rule or a useful generality with conviction, let your conviction show.

2. *Jesus was not content just to state principles. He followed through in two ways.*

First, His actions bespoke His beliefs. In extreme situations which were in flagrant violation of the principles He believed in, He was even capable of violence. (Note His actions toward merchants and moneychangers in the temple, John 2:14-16.) Of equal importance but less spectacular was His day-by-day consistency in living by the principles of love and truth He taught.

Next, He was always careful to give copious examples of the principles He enunciated. A tremendous proportion of His teaching time was spent in illustrations and stories to make His message crystal clear. (Is this true of you?) When He was asked, "Who is my neighbor?" He did not simply state the principle: "Your neighbor is anyone it is in your power to help." Rather, he told a delightful and ingenious story which made neighborliness come alive in the minds of His listeners (Luke 10:30-37).

3. *Jesus did not pry or nag at the lives of His disciples in applying the principles He taught.* He did a great deal of counseling, yet never set Himself up as a counselor. He simply let any who felt a need come and talk to Him about it. Except for occasionally chiding His disciples about their lack of faith (Matthew 6:30; 8:26; 16:8), He never "picked on" them for their imperfections. If, as in the case of the rich young ruler, someone asked Him a straight question as to what He should do next, Jesus did not hesitate to answer. *But He did not offer personal advice where it was not wanted.*

This is a very important distinction. It is probably as close as we can come to identifying how Jesus dealt with this matter of applying the truth to the practical circumstances of His pupils. He would state the truth—as grandly and inspirationally as possible. He would use imaginative illustrations as close as possible to the thinking patterns of those He was teaching. But He would *not* normally try to spell out the implications of the truth in terms of the detailed action of His hearers. "Go, and sin no more," He said to Mary Magdalene (John 8:11). But He did not interpret to the extent of saying, "If you are to sin no more, it will mean that you must do this and this and this. . . . " He knew she grasped the principle. Its outworking would be her own challenge and her own problem.

One's imagination can provide a great many oppor-

tunities for Jesus to have corrected those twelve
earthy men who were His disciples. Over a period of
three years' time must they not have sometimes gotten
on one another's nerves? Was there not one who
tended to lag behind the others? Were not some
habitually more talkative? Were there not a few more
sarcastic than the rest? Time and again Jesus could
have said, "Bartholomew, you are not being fair to
Thomas," or "Simon, give someone else a chance to
talk!" But He never did. Even when James and John
showed more than their share of personal ambition by
asking a special place in the kingdom (Mark 10:
35-40), Jesus did not rebuke them by name as individuals. He simply used it as an occasion to teach an
important general principle about the kingdom of
God. They made the application themselves.

Jesus spoke the truth. He made it clear enough to
be understood and vivid enough to be felt. Yet He did
not try to *impose* the truth; He let each pupil apply
it for himself, according to His conscience and understanding.

Because Jesus' teaching was almost exclusively to
adults, we cannot know for certain the differences He
would have made when conveying the truth to children. It seems likely, however, that He would have
modified His basic approach only enough to give the
young concrete samples of the *kinds* of action the
truth implied for their lives.

To help make the words of Jesus more real to us,
we should now and then turn from the majestic language of the King James Version to one of the newer
translations, one in modern speech. These are much
closer to the way Jesus would really sound if He were
ministering among us.

FROM SPECIFIC TO GENERAL AND BACK

In a way, pupils learn by getting a clear picture of a truth through examples. From the picture they are able to generalize and formulate a principle. Molded by the principle, they transform it again into a picture—the real life picture of their own real lives.

Teaching should be inspirational as well as informational; but most of all it should be life-changing, vital, transforming to the pupil, even revolutionary in its effects.

QUESTIONS

1. Explain how it is possible that people sometimes agree on principle but are far apart in practice.

2. What is the danger of teaching only broad principles?

3. What is the danger of spelling out completely for a student what his behavior should be in certain situations?

4. What differences would Jesus probably make in His parables if He were telling them today?

5. In what two ways did Jesus "follow through" with the principles He taught?

6. What can we learn from Jesus about giving advice?

7. Why is it difficult to assess Jesus' teaching methods with children?

8. What special value do modern-speech translations of the Bible have in the matter of applying principles?

—7—
POSITIVE OR NEGATIVE?

A certain talented tenor used to get nervous if a solo he was preparing required him to reach high A. Invariably he would ask his accompanist to transpose the selection downward so that his highest note would not be above G. The accompanist, a good musician herself, realized that the singer's problem was purely psychological. He could actually sing A—or higher—with ease. But the idea of having to sing no higher than G helped him to feel relaxed in front of an audience. One day, though she had rehearsed with him in the lower key he asked for, she switched back to the original, higher key when performance time came. And she did not tell the singer.

As she expected, he sang his solo with fine confidence, including a beautiful and bell-like high A. He thought he was only singing G, so he was supremely confident.

Every one of us probably has a similar quirk at one time or another. There is something we are actually quite able to do—except that we are afraid to attempt it. Self-confidence becomes the vital ingredient. If we can build enough of it we succeed at the undertaking; if not, we fail or never try at all.

LIMITED POWER

Some people call this the power of positive thinking. But no matter what you call it, the power is very real. There are many situations in life in which a positive attitude makes all the difference. But of course it would be foolhardy and dangerous to believe that positive thinking can accomplish everything by itself. The singer whose voice cannot reach high A will not have his throat transformed by the magic of suddenly believing the note is easy to hit. The actual ability must be there first. The ability *plus* the positive thinking—this is the winning combination.

But just a moment. How does the *ability* develop? Did not the singer somewhere along the line have to do some confident, positive thinking, even before his ability had been achieved? Didn't he at least have to believe that he could *learn* to sing well, that he could develop his talents? Without some kind of positivism he would never have started singing in public at all. And so with the exercise of many other similar talents.

REAL POWER

It seems, then, that a confident, optimistic approach is not just something to be added on when every other requirement is already in place. It is not only an ingredient, but also a catalyst. It has to be present to a certain extent before the other factors in human personality can function properly.

This train of thought has given rise to many books, articles, and speeches through the years. Any book display will show you several titles dealing with this "secret" of success. The authors state the idea in a wide variety of ways. Some recommend a simple optimism, always looking for and expecting the best to happen. Others regard the key as a simple denial of all that is evil or frightening. (Much of Mary Baker Eddy's "Christian Science" writing is extreme along this line.) Still others prescribe such formulas as saying to yourself, "I can do it, I can do it, I can do it."

How much good is this sort of thing? Positive thinking undoubtedly has power, but its power is limited. And this is where it is easy to go astray. There is power in *believing*, but there is infinitely more power in *believing what is true*. People who have illnesses that are based on psychological causes have many times been healed simply by being brought to a place of believing they would be healed. It made little difference whether they thought the agency of healing was a magic word, a favorite doctor, a supernatural dream, a miraculous drug, or the shrine of a "saint." They got better purely because they believed they would. But there are very obvious limits to this sort of thing. No one is likely to be healed of a serious organic disease simply because he believes —*unless the object of his belief actually has the power to heal him.*

Divine healing is, of course, not our subject in this chapter. The digression is only to illustrate that the power of positive thinking, or expectation, or optimism, or of faith by itself (independent of its object), is definitely and severely limited. Having accepted the fact that positivism is no cure-all, we may now profitably consider the ways it can actually benefit a Christian teacher.

BIBLE BASIS

Is all this talk about positive thinking simply a lot of modern theorizing, or is there a sound scriptural basis for it as a principle applicable to Christian teachers?

Paul wrote, "Whatsoever things are true ... honest ... just ... pure ... lovely ... of good report ... think on these things" (Philippians 4:8). According to the gospels, Jesus spent a great deal more of his time and energy in being "for" things than in being "against" things. In fact, this is one of the most conspicuous ways in which His teachings differ from those of the Old Testament prophets, and even from that of John the Baptist. The prophets before Him had spent much effort denouncing the evil deeds of the people. They indicted, condemned, threatened, warned. Jesus did some of this, too, as illustrated by His "Woe unto thee, Chorazin! ..." (Matthew 11:21). But by far the greater part of His teaching was positive. He never made condemnation His main business.

On the contrary, Jesus often went out of His way to register sympathy with people whom His disciples or others would have condemned. Consider for instance His attitude toward the Samaritan woman (John 4: 5-30), the little children who came to Him (Matthew 19:14), the adulteress brought to Him for judgment (John 8:3-11), the publican in the temple (Luke 18:10-14), and Zacchaeus (Luke 19:1-10).

Perhaps the list of things Jesus was against is just as long as the list of things He was for—but He did not spend as much time dealing with the "against" list. The things against which He was the most out-spoken were not the traditional sins so despised by the righteous of His day. Rather His greatest con-demnation was directed at such things as self-righteous-ness, hypocrisy, mechanical piety, religious commer-cialism, and irreverence. He only rarely made anyone's wickedness the subject of a sermon or a parable. One exception is the story of the unjust servant (Matthew 18:23-25).

Some of the things He praised were neighborliness (the good Samaritan, Luke 10:30-37), perseverance in prayer (Luke 11:5-8), humility (the publican in the temple, Luke 18:10-14), action rather than words (the two sons, Matthew 21:28-31), and generosity in giving (the widow's mite, Luke 21:1-4). Other passages show His admiration of such qualities as unselfishness, repentance, industry, and faith. In the main, His tone was always that of advocate rather than prosecutor.

Was there perhaps less evil to condemn in the world of Jesus' time? No, indeed! It was an age filled with the evils of slavery, political intrigue and corruption, racial and national prejudices, religious intolerance, unjust courts, burdensome taxation, and factionalism of all kinds. He did not have to look far for evils to condemn. Why, then, did He say so little about these evils? Or, in the manner of thinking of our generation, why did he not "demonstrate" or organize protests against the tremendous social evils of His time?

WHY JESUS WAS POSITIVE

The reason Jesus did not spend His time attacking the bad things He saw around Him is the same reason you as a Christian teacher should not give most of your energy to fighting the bad things in your own community. It boils down to this: The person who is mostly "against" things is actually letting the enemy determine the nature and timing of the battle. To be "against" is to fight back, to respond, to *re*act instead of to act. Satan would have liked nothing better than to keep Jesus occupied in fighting back at attacks of Satan's own making. If he could have got Jesus to spend His time lashing out at such injustices as the Roman oppression, he would have been quite happy. But Jesus always brushed such temptations quickly aside. (See the story of the tribute money, Mark 12:14-17.)

It is an old debating trick to try to get your opponent to spend his time discussing the issues *you* have raised. That way he will have no chance to present his own case properly.

This is the great power of positivism. Affirmation is always stronger than denial, for it is direct action rather than mere reaction. The positivist always holds the initiative—and usually controls the atmosphere.

BE AFFIRMATIVE

To you as a Sunday school teacher this principle can mean a great deal. Most fundamentally of all, you should see to it that your enthusiasm for those ideas you *favor* is much stronger and more conspicuous than your enthusiasm against those ideas you deplore. The net result—constructive teaching—will leave a better taste and greater effect than destructive teaching.

Of course there are many cases in which it is impossible to be effectively "for" anything without being conspicuously "against" something else. You will never entirely eliminate the negative from your teaching. What is called for is a sense of proper emphasis. Accentuate the positive and you are on the right track.

In matters of doctrine, this means, for instance, that you should strive to motivate your pupils more by the promise of heaven than by the threat of hell, though hell is very real. Educational studies have repeatedly shown that, whether on the large eternal scale or the small hour-by-hour one, pupils are far more successfully motivated through their rewards than through their punishments.

One implication is that you should not allow much class time to be spent on derogatory remarks about another church or religion. "But if we don't attack false cults," someone says, "how will people know they are wrong?"

INNOCULATE AGAINST ERROR

The best antidote for falsehood is simply truth. There is such a thing as giving so much time to the study of various false doctrines that one hardly knows what is true doctrine. And it is always impossible to predict just what variety of false doctrine your pupils are likely to encounter next. In other words, you cannot successfully teach against all the possible falsehoods. You *can* concentrate on the truth—to such an extent that your pupils will recognize falsehood instantly when they come across it.

To sum up, both negative and positive attitudes are necessary. The one implies the other. However, it is healthier for a teacher—and much closer to the example of Jesus—to emphasize what you are *for* rather than what you are against. Be a protagonist rather than an antagonist. Sponsor action, not reaction. Do not resist progress, but try to guide it in order to be sure it will be *genuine* progress.

Perhaps the most important positivism of all is in the teacher's attitude toward not merely his subject matter, but his pupils. Be sure your pupils feel that you are *for* them at all times. If you cannot be for everything they do, pick those things you can approve, and let your approval be known. Learners, especially younger learners, always have a very great need to feel that someone is on their side. And there is no better feeling for a pupil than to know his *teacher* is truly with him.

FOR OTHERS

A leading theologian of today has made a significant contribution to theology with the emergence of a view of Jesus which saw Him as "the man for others." Some other theologians have carried this thought on to absurd extremes. And of course Jesus was much more than simply a "man for others." However, though not the whole truth, this truth about Jesus is certainly one of His outstanding characteristics. He was always *for*. He transformed others by being and doing, not by condemning what they were or did. And what is more, He set a pattern which as Christian teachers we must do our best to follow all the way.

QUESTIONS

1. Describe the "power of positive thinking."

2. Give two examples of cases where Jesus was "for" people whom others were generally against.

3. Explain how a negative attitude lacks iniative.

4. Which is a stronger motivation for pupils: the prospect of reward, or the threat of punishment?

5. Why is it somewhat impracticable to study false doctrines?

6. Explain the expression, "the man for others."

—8—
SPECTACULAR OR SUBTLE?

A missionary stood preaching the gospel in the open air in a little village of Liberia, West Africa. No one before had ever held a Christian meeting there, and the villagers listened and looked with great curiosity. For an hour the sermon went on—a careful step-by-step explanation of the Biblical plan of salvation. Impressed by the careful attention he was obviously receiving, and hoping to make his presentation still clearer, the missionary ended his message by offering to answer any questions. Immediately one of the African men spoke up. "I've been wondering all the time you've been speaking," he said, "wherever did you get those marvelous shoes you're wearing?"

WHY FOOLISH QUESTIONS?

You who teach in Sunday school know that you do not need to go to Africa to hear irrelevant questions asked. Hardly an invitation for questions goes by, it seems, without someone's asking about a matter you didn't have in mind at all.

Does this merely mean that human beings are somewhat illogical and don't listen well? No, there is more to it. Here are some of the reasons your pupil may have asked the question you find so irrelevant.

1. *Perhaps he simply has not understood what you were trying to say.* Communications experts remind us

that all transfer of thought from one person to another must use some sort of code. That is, the thought must be reduced to symbols, transmitted, received, and decoded into thought again. There are possibilities of breakdown at any of the steps in this process.

2. *Perhaps his interests and goals are somewhat different from yours.* The pupil may not know the purpose you have in mind; he may be interested in some other purpose entirely. He will seize on some thought, possibly insignificant to you, and pursue it in a direction other than you intended.

3. *Perhaps he has been led astray by side elements of which you are not even aware.* This was in large part the case with the story of the missionary's shoes. That missionary soon learned to begin his sermons with a short explanation of who he was and where he came from, giving enough information to dispel some of the curiosity about him personally. Then his hearers would give more attention to his message and less to his appearance.

Parts of the communication problem (No. 1 above) are dealt with in various chapters of this book. The differences in aim (No. 2 above) are commented on in chapter 4. So let us turn to a brief consideration of *unconscious teaching*, the problem area associated with No. 3 above.

JESUS TAUGHT DELIBERATELY

Was it a problem for Jesus? We can answer with an unequivocal *no*. The Master knew what He was doing through each step of His ministry, and many are the books which have pointed with awe to the sound educational principles he employed—some of which would not be discovered till centuries later.

This is not to say Jesus always got the responses He wanted. He did not *want* the rich young ruler to turn away (Mark 10:22). He did not *want* the Pharisees to resent His healing people on the Sabbath (Luke 13:14). He knew that some would react to His words and His works with antipathy, even hatred. The free will of men will always mean that some will respond badly. But surely Jesus was at all times fully aware of the potential effects of all His actions. His predictions prove it.

AIM PAST THE ACCIDENTAL

To us mere mortal teachers, it may seem unfair to say that we should be like Christ in this respect. We are so far from being omniscient as He was. But, if it is unrealistic to aspire to a perfect understanding of all the effects of our teaching, at least we should aspire to understand as many of those effects as possible. Some very good teaching has sometimes been done "by accident" in the experience of many of us. But it could have been even better if we had understood exactly what was taking place.

Elsewhere we have called all education "guided experience." Another way of putting it is to say that education is *organized learning*. And the teacher is the organizer. In fact, it can be argued that this is the major contribution a teacher has to make to the learning process. He must organize the curriculum, his own thoughts, the methods to be used, the physical environment, and the interests and activities of the pupils.

The better these factors are organized, the less unconscious teaching will leak through. Remember, it is not necessarily a matter of wanting to *eliminate* the content of the unconscious teaching, but just to make it conscious. If learning of any kind is taking place (and it takes place almost continuously with some age groups) , the teacher most certainly should know it.

At this point let us hasten to add that it is *not* necessary for the *pupils* to understand all the processes being used. Unconscious *teaching* is far from being ideal, but unconscious *learning* is fine in most cases. In fact, some kinds of learning will take place far better if the learner does not realize he is learning.

WHAT YOU NEED TO KNOW

"Knowledge is power," goes the old saying, and this is particularly true for a teacher. If he is to organize and guide the learning process, he needs to know and know and know. To use a formula of the kind popular with salesmen:

1. Know your product.
2. Know your prospect.
3. Know your procedures.

For you, the Christian Sunday school teacher, your "product" is salvation and the Christian way of life. Your "prospect" is the pupil entrusted to your care. Your "procedures" are all of those means and methods by which the prospect is led to accept the product.

SALESMANSHIP IS INADEQUATE

A few years ago it became very popular to speak of spreading the gospel in terms of modern merchandising, and some Christians began to think of evangelism purely in terms of salesmanship. Though it is clear there are points of strong similarity, there are also important points of difference. In what ways is it wrong to think of the gospel as something to be "sold"?

1. *The salesman's motivation is very often* (but admittedly not always) *his drive for personal success.* Such a motivation (as in the thought, "I want to be thought of as a *good* teacher") can be disastrous for you, if for no other reason than that it is un-Christlike. Jesus' motivation always centered on His pupils, never on Himself. Even in His Gethsemane prayers, the disciples were His major concern.

2. *The salesman's concept is too often built around a short-range goal.* Even if he is alive to repeat business, he is likely to see it one sale at a time. And each sale is a specific event identifiable as to when and what. You as a teacher cannot look at your work that way. It is difficult or impossible to say to yourself on any given day, "I have accomplished my goal."

3. *The salesman usually gets his rewards as he goes along.* You may receive many satisfactions as your teaching progresses, but your major reward—the heavenly—awaits the end of your teaching career.

4. *The salesman's work is to a certain extent irreversible.* Most sales, once made, are not cancelable at the whim of the purchaser. He has the product, like it or not, and his economic commitment may force him to keep it sometimes against his wishes. As a teacher, your work is far from being this kind of one-way street. An act of will, a mere change of attitude on the part of a pupil, and his commitment can be revoked.

The common element in the above contrasts is the constant and selfless concern of the Sunday school teacher. Always alert, always at it, always thinking beyond the moment and beyond self—these are the marks of the Master-teacher and of those who carry on His work.

TWO KINDS OF PROGRESS

If the teacher's task is such a continuous one, it is plain that he cannot conduct it always at a high pitch of drama and emotion. Emphasis cannot be truly continuous any more than mountains can exist without valleys. A pupil actually makes progress in two different ways:

1. *By specially vivid experiences.* These are the occasions he will later look back on and say, "I remember what an impression that made on me." They are red-letter days that stand out. Maturity and perception take a sudden leap upward. The pupil is never the same again.

In the realm of the spiritual, such experiences have a very important place. We distinguish the born-again experience of each believer as being such a revolutionary, life-changing step; we also recognize that the infilling of the Holy Spirit (as in Acts 2) can be an equally transforming experience. Other specific high points in the Christian life are perhaps not so easily defined, but may nevertheless be very real. An act of dedication, the sudden thrill of answered prayer, a special sense of divine presence—these and many more kinds of sacred times make deep impressions from which we learn.

2. *By slow, steady growth.* This is in contrast to the isolated, vivid experiences. Just as a flower develops by gradual changes which over any short period are hardly perceptible, so the pupil learns in part by a slowly unfolding understanding, "precept upon

precept, line upon line, here a little and there a little."

In the pupil's spiritual life, this kind of growth is brought about by the countless small decisions of life—the temptations rejected, the acts of unselfishness, the times of prayer, the daily Bible reading, the whole list of self-disciplines of all sizes.

This is also the area in which the pupil's learning is the least conscious. And it is the area in which a teacher actually spends the most time. He does not flash, nor hammer, nor sparkle here. He pushes with an even pressure, he glows softly, he quietly suggests.

SLOW BUT SURE

Was not this the kind of gentle teaching in which Jesus spent the most time? Of course there were the red-letter days—the Transfiguration, the Sermon on the Mount, the more spectacular miracles. But there were also the hours of patient teaching of the disciples as the group moved about together. This was subtle teaching. Not subtle in the sense of subterfuge or deceit, but subtle in the sense of lacking fanfare. And subtle most of all in that the disciples were probably not aware of the extent of Christ's teaching in their lives.

There is no evidence that any of the disciples took extensive notes on Jesus' teachings as they went along. The gospels seem to have been written from recollections afterwards, prompted by the Holy Spirit. Only looking back did the disciples perceive the true pattern and significance of the truths their Lord had taught.

NEVER A MERE LURE

For convenience, let us use the term "spectacular"

to refer to the deep-impression, special occasion, red-letter day kind of teaching, and use the term "subtle" to refer to the quieter, more constant kind. In Jesus' ministry, a great deal of the "spectacular" centered around His miracles, so let us consider for a moment the relationship between His miracles and His teaching.

The most important principle here is that Jesus never used a miracle as any kind of "bait" to get people to listen to His words. Of course the miracles unquestionably had the effect of "bait" to some people, even though Jesus was not deliberately using them for this purpose. There are few if any people in the world who are not interested in or moved by a miracle. The supernatural is a tremendous attraction always. And where the supernatural is present, whether in Jesus' time or our own, crowds will gather.

VIEWS OF THE SUPERNATURAL

For the most part Jesus accepted this fact. But one of the puzzles of the gospels has always been that some of the time He specifically asked those He healed not to spread the news abroad; other times He made no such request; still other times He encouraged them to broadcast what had been done for them. Why the differences? A possible answer is that in His early ministry He did not want to be followed just by crowds interested *only* in the miracles. Once He was established and accepted as a teacher, this was no longer an issue. It is as if He were saying, "I have no objection to being known as a teacher who also heals, but I do not want to be known as just a healer who also teaches."

Jesus knew that people's motives sort them out.

A person who is attracted only by the miraculous element *may* turn out not to be interested in anything else. And He knew that in the long run the *subtle,* not just the *spectacular,* kind of learning was necessary if His purposes were to be accomplished.

The same is true today. Many a church has sprung up composed of people who were attracted mostly or altogether to the spectacular. But very few of these have matured into permanently strong, healthy churches unless the congregations have soon begun an interest in steady, long-range teaching. Of course this does not mean the miraculous has no longer been present at all.

The reason healing was so much more prominent in the teaching ministry of Jesus is not because He "used" it to attract people. Rather He simply let it function in perspective with the rest of His work, "showing the Father" to the world. In His mind, healing was just one aspect of ministry. Because He was so perfectly attuned to God by faith, healing was much more common in His ministry than in ours; but His teaching was likewise much greater than ours.

SYNTHETICS ON THE SCENE

The "spectacular" in modern organized religion takes in much more than the miraculous. It takes in whatever is highly unusual, dramatic, or attention-getting. It is inevitable, though pathetic, that many people from whom the miraculous has departed strive to substitute a human "spectacular" element of their own making. The result is sometimes a kind of perpetual gimmickry, employed in an attempt to catch or hold interest.

Do Sunday school teachers use such tactics? Yes,

unfortunately, sometimes they do. Have you ever found yourself including in a class session some novel demonstration, game, story, or contest just because the class would be fascinated—even though you knew it had little if anything to do with the lesson subject? Most of us plead guilty.

AIDS SHOULD POINT, NOT SHOUT

Where does the legitimate use of audio-visual aids leave off and shallow gimmickry begin? There can be no clear-cut line of division; however, for your own class situation, ask yourself these questions about any aid or novel item you use:

1. Is it closely related not merely to my general subject but also to the specific point I am trying to get across?

2. Is it the best possible way I could make use of the time it takes?

3. Is it likely to call pupils' attention more to the truth it illustrates than to its own novelty?

If you can answer yes to all three questions, you probably have something you can use to good advantage, not a mere gimmick.

The unifying principle in these three measures is: The more conspicuous a teaching method is as a method, the greater the chance that it is actually unsuitable. Method is something like background music: when it is performing its function best, no one especially notices it is there. If you fall noisily to the floor as a means of illustrating what happened to Goliath when David's stone struck him, you run the risk that your class will remember not how shocked the Philistines must have looked but rather how silly *you* looked. However, if you can manage to keep the class thinking only about the David and Goliath story, fine.

Can any visual aids actually be considered "subtle" teaching in the sense we have been discussing? Probably, if they are simple and convenient enough. Complex gadgetry invariably calls attention to itself, and all the more so if some malfunction develops. Today's trend is more and more toward convenience of use. The manufacturers of projector equipment of all kinds, for example, are trying very hard to produce machines which are genuinely easy to use.

Actually, a visual aid must not only *be* convenient; it must also *appear* convenient to the casual observer. Even the simplest piece of equipment will call attention to itself and away from the lesson if the teacher is fussing over it with a worried look. For this reason there is such a thing as too much variety in visual aid types for a given classroom. No teacher is equally proficient in the use of all types. If he keeps changing all the time, he has no chance to really get to know any type very well. Also, pupils are easily distracted by the use of a new and unfamiliar machine or style of presentation. When teacher and pupils are pretty well used to, say, using filmstrips, they reach the point where they are hardly aware of the mechanics of the thing—hence are able to give more attention to the application.

The visual aids Jesus used were very simple. In many cases we have no way of knowing whether or not He was actually within sight or touching distance of some of the objects He used. But they were almost invariably things that were readily observable in the disciples' daily lives. He spoke of lilies, a grapevine, a fig tree, a penny, a beam and a splinter, fish, foxes, salt, lamps, and many other concrete objects.

THE OLD RELIABLES

For you as a teacher, the simplest visual aids are probably the following:

1. *An actual object.* This can be anything—a pencil, a bell, a clock, a telescope, a loaf of bread. With some meditation you will find there is something to be learned from almost every object in the world. If the object is rare or awkward to handle, a picture or sketch of it will often do.

2. *Flash cards.* These can be much trouble to prepare, but their use in class is very simple and uncluttered. A set can be made for almost any subject, in any size. In complexity they can range from professional-type artwork to a few simple lines.

3. *Chalkboard.* This is probably the most universal aid in American Sunday schools today. Its use involves no measurable expense. Any person who can write is able to use it. Nothing need be carried to and from the classroom. Spur-of-the-moment improvization is especially easy.

4. *Flannel board.* This is the aid that almost revolutionized Sunday school teaching a generation ago. Preparation can be time-consuming, but presentations have almost no limits except the imagination of the teacher. Costs are moderate, sizes vary (and many are too small).

This list is deliberately limited to those aids common enough to meet the requirements of the "subtle" approach; they are unlikely to call any great attention to themselves. They are listed in what the author considers to be their order of simplicity of use, with the easiest first. Your idea of this order may be different.

The spectacular or the subtle? Here is another

question that can be answered only by appealing for moderation. The dramatic, supercharged moment may have genuine teaching value by making a thought strike with great force. But the quiet, steady, subtle kind of teaching may overtake the flamboyant variety even as the tortoise did the hare. The one may give the velocity of a racer, the other a carrying power that is geared for the hills.

QUESTIONS

1. Why do pupils sometimes ask irrelevant questions in class?

2. Give a simplified definition of education.

3. Discuss the "product," the "prospect," and the "procedures" for a Sunday school teacher.

4. How is Christian evangelism *unlike* salesmanship?

5. Cite examples in your own life or the lives of your pupils of the two kinds of spiritual progress. Cite examples from Jesus' ministry.

6. Why did Jesus give different, sometimes opposite, instructions to people whom He healed?

7. What is the unifying principle in measuring the use of audio visuals or teaching methods?

8. What are the simplest visual aids for teachers?

—9—
SCHEDULE OR IMPROVISE?

"It's not fair," said a junior high Sunday school teacher. "I was at Susan's house until after ten on Saturday night—and she admitted to me she hadn't yet prepared her Sunday school lesson. But when Sunday morning came she did a wonderful job of teaching! I had to go into her room to borrow some chalk— and you should have seen the eager interest on the faces of her students. How does she do it? I am sure she didn't have more than a half-hour's preparation, while *I* worked all week on my lesson. Some people just have a natural talent!"

PREPARATION PATTERNS VARY

We all know teachers who get by with very little preparation. And they are not necessarily all poor teachers, either. In fact, some of us have noticed that the better a teacher is, the *less* time he often seems to spend in preparation! How can this be so?

Every book and every adviser on Sunday school matters tell us that a teacher should conscientiously spend as much time as possible preparing. Yet no one knows what is the average number of hours per week spent by an average Sunday school teacher in preparing his Sunday school lesson. Neither do we know the *ideal* number of hours. But we can be sure that there is a very wide range of extremes in the amount of time spent. A few give the lesson some attention every day throughout the week. More give a brief portion of several evenings to their preparation. Some depend upon a concentrated cram session on Saturday night. And a few (dare we say it?) make do with a brief glance at the lesson on Sunday morning.

PREPARATION IS PART OF TEACHING

The time available for the Christian education of our pupils in Sunday school is woefully short. The least any conscientious teacher can do is to see to it that he is reasonably well prepared to teach any given session. He should understand that he assumes this obligation when he agrees to be a Sunday school teacher. An increasing number of churches make use of a kind of "teacher's covenant" which each teacher signs when he becomes a member of the teaching staff. Among other things, it contains a promise of regular and adequate lesson preparation.

But what is "adequate"? In terms of results, it is that amount and kind of preparation which will produce in a class those learning experiences appropriate to the class and to the curricular material being used. In terms of the teacher himself, adequate preparation is whatever it takes to give the teacher a genuine readiness (spiritually and intellectually) to produce satisfactory learning experiences in his pupils.

The variation in the amounts of time teachers spend getting their lessons ready are found not only between individual teachers, but within the individual experience of any given teacher. In other words, you spend more time preparing some lessons than others. A new teacher may at first follow a different pattern of preparation than the one he settles down to later on. A veteran who has taught in one department for thirty years or so may not prepare today in the same way nor for the same length of time that he used to do. Why so much variation?

REASONS FOR DIFFERENCES

One reason is the variety of importance attached to the activity. Some teachers simply take their teaching more seriously than others. Furthermore, an individual teacher may fluctuate in his attitude toward teaching—and the fluctuations will show in the amount of time he gives to his preparation. Perhaps you have never thought of your preparation time as being a kind of thermometer of your spiritual condition, but it may well be.

A second factor which accounts for a great deal of the variety in preparation time is the actual teaching ability of the teacher concerned. A teacher with a high degree of ability may find it easy to think of just the right illustrations, visual aids, stories, and other procedures to make his lesson interesting and effective. Meanwhile, another teacher whose ability is less—whether by inexperience or lack of training— may spend many hours devising the right kind of approach to use for a particular lesson. Variations in ability are part of the great picture of human variety. Not all of us are the same.

A third consideration which will affect the amount of time necessary for the preparation of a particular lesson is the nature of the material itself. (This is quite apart from how familiar the material is to the teacher; we shall consider this aspect separately.) Some lessons just require more time in the mental "mill" than do others. The kind of truth being taught, the number and length of Scripture passages used, the availability or scarcity of illustrations, the simplicity or complexity of visual aids needed: all will affect the time necessary to get the teacher ready for the class.

A fourth factor—and perhaps most determinative of all—is the kind and amount of preparation the teacher has already done previously.

Preparation is of two kinds: general and specific. Specific preparation is the work and thought which goes into your getting ready for a certain class with a certain group of people at a certain time. You are thinking about the people, the place, and the time as you prepare. This is the kind of preparation we mean when we say, "I'd better go home and prepare my Sunday school lesson now." General preparation is much broader. It includes:

1. Your background of life experience in all areas that are related in any way to the subject matter being considered.

2. Your knowledge of the Bible and Christian principles of all kinds.

3. Your knowledge and skill in the use of teaching methods.

4. Your record or memory of other lessons or occasions on which you taught truths of similar kind to that now being considered.

The richer the background of your general preparation, the less time your specific preparation is likely to take. Fritz Kreisler, the famous violinist, was once asked, "How much time do you spend practicing?" The old virtuoso smiled. "I used to practice," he said. "Now I play." No doubt this was an oversimplification, but we all understand what he meant. His technique had reached the point where he was in a more-or-less constant state of readiness to perform.

None of us has such a complete knowledge of the Bible that he is likely to be ready to teach any lesson at any time without specific preparation. But it is true that the greater your store of knowledge and experience, the less time you will need to get ready for a particular occasion.

THE TEMPTATION OF EXPERIENCE

There is a great danger here. If you are a teacher who has been at it a long time, you are sure to be tempted to feel that your background of general preparation is enough to pull you through without giving much specific time to next Sunday's lesson. And it is true you could probably "get by" much better than a less experienced teacher.

But look at it this way. Your former investment of study time can provide you with dividends in either of two ways. You can draw a "bonus" by excusing yourself from spending as much time in preparation as you used to. Or you can pass the bonus on to your pupils by using the time to sharpen up your preparation far beyond the bare minimum needed. You can search out that more appropriate illustration, that obscure Scripture passage, that extra bit of Jewish lore, that finer diagram—and be a better teacher than ever. Don't merely measure yourself against the novice teacher; measure yourself against yourself, and try perpetually to improve.

Have you ever heard a teacher who has approximately the same things to say, no matter what the week's lesson topic is? Unfortunately, such teachers are all too common. It is as if they look at the lesson material, pull out of their mental file the group of canned thoughts which are closest to it, and talk away. Such a teacher may communicate very well—until he exhausts his dozen or so pre-prepared subjects. Then his teaching becomes simply a week-by-week rehash of old material, no matter what the lesson says. Beware! Check yourself as to this particular fault. And keep in mind that this is a flaw most often found in the *experienced*, not the inexperienced, teacher.

JESUS' PREPARATION

What can we learn about a teacher's preparation from the life of Jesus? Because the circumstances under which Jesus taught were very different from those of the average Sunday school of today, we must use some imagination to derive guidance from the Lord's example. Suppose you as a teacher were to study thoroughly not just the lesson for one Sunday, nor for a month, nor for a quarter, but for three years' worth of teaching. Imagine that you prepared *all* the lessons before you taught even the *first* one. You mastered the material, knew the Scripture references, understood the principles and the methods to be used. Imagine you had all this bottled up inside you, just waiting to get out. Now, suppose further that you decided you would teach the lessons not in a rigidly fixed order, but would be guided by circumstances and opportunities. That is, when a certain chance presented itself, you would "pull out" the lesson most appropriately connected with it, and pass that lesson along to your pupils.

The analogy may be rather crude, but this is something like what Jesus did. Of course He was not following a rigid framework of subject matter as we do in most of our Sunday school teaching. He had no formal curriculum; as far as we know, He had no regular "school hours." Therefore we find no record of His preparing a specific lesson—because His lessons were not scheduled in the ordinary sense. His preparation was almost entirely in the area we have called "general preparation."

There are, however, examples of His specific preparation for some particular experiences He was about to undergo. His baptism by John (Matthew 3:16) was preparation for His temptations in the wilderness (Matthew 4:1-11). His agony in the Garden (Luke 22:44) was preparation for the suffering He was to endure during the following hours. And throughout His ministry there were times of special prayer which provided a sort of spiritual charge before He undertook some difficult aspect of ministry. But these were *spiritual* preparation, not *curricular* preparation.

The fact remains that as to the content and method of His teaching, Jesus' preparation was almost entirely of the general kind. But what a tremendous background of knowledge He had built up! In His messages He quoted from an enormous spread of Old Testament writings. And He was obviously a keen observer of human nature and culture. He told stories based on universal human experience. He spoke of a wedding (the ten virgins, Matthew 25:1-13), a jealous brother (the prodigal son, Luke 15:25-30), a housewife who misplaced some money in the house (the lost coin, Luke 15:8, 9), a farmer and his risks (the sower, Matthew 13:3-8).

FACTORS IN PLANNING

To a considerable extent, the specific lessons Jesus

taught seem to have been inspired by coincidental occasions. However, though He did not teach according to a rigid timetable, it is noticeable that the sequence of His teachings was not entirely random, either. The order of what He taught appears to have been guided by at least three considerations:

1. He took advantage of seasons, special events, chance contacts, spontaneous circumstances. Though as a Sunday school teacher you cannot very well follow such a "free curriculum," yet you should keep in mind that there is great value in relating your subject matter to those things that are already high in the interest and concern of your listeners.

2. Jesus took into consideration the moral maturity of His listeners. He taught His disciples matters that were far more complex and subtle than those that He taught to the crowds in general. And, as His disciples progressed in knowledge, He moved on to things they might not have responded to at first. For example, the detailed prophecies of Matthew 24 would surely have been even more baffling to His disciples if the Lord had given them at the beginning of His ministry.

As a teacher, *you* must also take into consideration the level of Christian development of your pupils. If your class is composed largely of new converts, your handling of certain subject matter should certainly be in different order from what it would be if they were all "old saints."

3. Jesus also recognized that there are logical "learning sets" of knowledge or perception. Some sequences of presentation are more sensible than others. First He told the parable of the lost sheep,

then of the lost coin, then of the lost son (Luke 15).
This gave a kind of climactic order to the truth He
was presenting. It implies that the father-son relationship is a higher and more ultimate form of describing the believer's position before God than the
metaphor of the sheep or the coin.

Always watch for the best and most reasonable
sequence of presentation as you teach. Proceed from
the known to the unknown, from what is accepted
to what has not yet been accepted, from the ordinary
to the extraordinary. Teaching is like leading someone along a path. Its segments cannot very well be
traversed in a random or accidental order; they should
fit together in a smooth sequence just as one foot
follows the other.

HOW RIGID A PLAN?

Jesus' own life was planned "from the foundation
of the world." Yet, except for its final events, it
shows little evidence of a strict timetable. Jesus made
few if any appointments. He seems to have been
very busy, yet without being hurried and without
struggling to meet deadlines.

His attitude toward planning can be summed up in
two ways: In personal matters, He taught "Take ...
no thought for the morrow ... " (Matthew 6:34).
But in matters of duty He taught long-range fore-
thought and careful calculation. (See the parable of
the talents, Matthew 25:14-30; the parables of the
tower builder and warring king, Luke 14:28-33.)

Planning ahead is largely a matter of thought. And
the gospels relate the *actions* of Jesus, not His
thoughts. Therefore it is difficult for us to assess
just how much advance planning our Lord may have

done day by day. However, two important principles
emerge—and are confirmed by the later attitudes of
the Apostle Paul toward planning:

1. Plan a strategy. This may include your goals,
a tentative time schedule of action, and basic decisions about methods to be used.

2. Apply flexible tactics. This includes adaptation
to special conditions, modifying, adjusting, probing,
ever searching for the best and highest way to present
the truth and make it real.

Another way of stating these principles is to say
it is always a good idea first to have a plan, and
second, to be willing to deviate from the plan as
circumstances may require. Actually, this seems to be
a sound method even for determining the leading of
the Lord most of the time. To have a plan implies
that you have decided what you intend to do—if you
are left free to do it. To be willing to modify the plan
implies that you recognize that no plan is necessarily
foolproof and perfect, but is subject to change or to
last-minute instructions from your Master.

A noted New Testament example of these principles
is found in the story of Paul's response to the
Macedonian call. He had decided, based upon his
own evaluation of the situation, that he should go
and evangelize Bithynia (Acts 16:7). This was his
proposed plan of action. If the Holy Spirit had not
intervened he would have pursued it—and could have
done so in confidence that he was in line with God's
will. However, the Holy Spirit did intervene and gave
him a vision of a man of Macedonia. Paul therefore
revised his original plan and adjusted to the new
guidance he had received.

USING THE UNEXPECTED

Though perhaps less conspicuously, Jesus seems to have used this basic approach in His attitude toward teaching situations. He always had some underlying goal or "plan of action." But He was ever willing to adjust to circumstances, to alter His original plan, to seize on some new and unexpected opportunity. The story of His ministry might almost be called, "Making the Most of Life's Interruptions."

In similar fashion, the effective Sunday school teacher will always *have a plan.* He will know what he intends to do, and he will proceed to do it— unless there are unexpected and overriding considerations that make it necessary to change. But if such considerations do arise, the effective teacher will be ready—even eager—to adapt to the new circumstances.

If you, when teaching, find you must often change your plan of approach while actually conducting the session, *this is not necessarily a sign of poor planning.* Successful teaching—for you as well as for your Lord— is a blend of careful planning and sensitive opportunism.

QUESTIONS

1. Explain the meaning of "general preparation."

2. Explain the meaning of "specific preparation."

3. Upon which is an experienced teacher tempted to lean too much?

4. Which kind of preparation did Jesus apparently use most?

5. In Jesus' extemporaneous teaching style, what considerations apparently helped determine the order of presentation of His teachings?

6. How rigidly should a teaching plan be followed?

7. What should be a teacher's attitude toward interruptions?

— 10 —
IMPART OR IMPLANT?

Billie Davis, well-known missionary, speaker, writer, and Sunday school specialist, had an underprivileged childhood among migrant workers. She tells of how, at one western camp for poverty-stricken families, a nearby bakery used to distribute day-old bread to help the needy. A truck would be sent among the tents, and a man would stand on the back and toss out the loaves to the scrambling children. Mrs. Davis says that though she grabbed for the free bread along with the other boys and girls, in her heart she hated the bakery, the truck, the bread, and the man who threw it. Why? Well, in her words, "Because they made me feel like a chicken." Like the rest, she accepted what was given—because she and her family needed it. But she resented the *way* it was given.

Her account of the new world she found when, later than most children, Billie Davis was able to begin attending public school and Sunday school, has inspired teachers by the thousand. To her it was a tremendous lift to find teachers who did not offer knowledge to children with the attitude, "I'm going to give you something you need, and you ought to be grateful." Rather, she says, most of them seemed to take the attitude, "Little girl, threadbare or not, you have in you possibilities for things worthwhile and fine. I want to help you find and develop them."

Many of us have had the good fortune to know at least a few such teachers in our own experience. And how powerful is their influence in our lives! May we mean as much to the pupils we now teach Sunday by Sunday. We are not making handouts; we are helping pupils grow.

ANY LIMIT?

One often hears it said that no teacher can lift his pupils to a level above that which he has himself achieved. Perhaps this is true if one thinks of the teacher as doing the "lifting" entirely himself. But actually it is the pupil's efforts as well that determine his progress. The limits of inadequate teaching are certainly a handicap, but fortunately they do not put an iron ceiling over the head of the aspiring pupil. You have only to think of some of the best musicians you know (pianists, for example) to realize that very often a person may become more proficient in his field than the one who taught him.

This is the heart of our subject for this chapter. A teacher *can* help pupils to attainments beyond his own. Much as a parent often yearns to see a child move forward to things the parent himself never reached, so a dedicated teacher should aspire to help members of his class to surpass him in knowledge or zeal or both.

AMPLIFIED EFFECTS

Jesus said, "He that believeth on me, the works that I do shall he do also; and greater works than these shall he do; because I go unto my Father" (John 14:12). This reveals that our Lord had in mind that those He taught should go on to greater things than even He had showed them. "Take what I have given you and go on with it—not merely perpetuating, but expanding." This was His attitude, and it should be the attitude of every Christian teacher.

Far from belittling a teacher's importance, this concept really means that a teacher's effect upon a pupil may in the long run be greater than anyone can imagine. Compare it with the work of a harbor pilot whose task requires him to leave an outgoing ship and return to shore. "Hold her on the course I have set until you pass the outer buoy," he says to the helmsman. "This course will clear the obstacles." And away goes a ship to ports the pilot will never see. But any error he may have made when giving a heading would be greatly magnified by the movement of the vessel and could lead to a serious disaster at a distance.

Or think of an investor who puts money into a small venture which later becomes fantastically successful. His rewards may be hundreds of times his investment, but they will always be *in proportion to his investment*. A couple that invested $100 of their savings with Henry Ford in his beginnings later sold their interest for $50,000. If they had managed to scrape up $200 to invest, it would have brought $100,000 when they sold. Here our point is not the amount of gain, but how much the initial investment determines it.

In the same way, what a teacher can accomplish in pupils' lives becomes amplified by time and distance until it is enormous. The influence you wield in your classroom is a veritable "power-steering" system in which a slight touch on your part can make a tremendous difference.

STARTING UP THE FUTURE

Of course no teacher can possibly foresee with accuracy all the results of his teaching. You are not dealing with the predictables of metal machinery but with the complex personalities of people—each of whom can by an act of will reject or accept your efforts. Your job is to create or increase the *possibility* of the right kind of development in pupils.

Here is another great quandary for teachers. Your real interest is in the end product—Christian character in the lives of pupils. Yet you have no direct control of the end product; you work in the *now*, separated from your goal by not only time but by many freewill decisions that will be made completely without your direct advice. To put it in pessimistic terms, you as a teacher are always starting something you cannot possibly finish.

Your job is not to *satisfy* people, but to *stimulate* them. You must not just put ideas into minds, but also draw ideas out. You plant, so to speak, a grain of truth around which the pupil may build his own pearl. And only he can produce that particular pearl. Your part is to start the process, initiate the chain of circumstances, even introduce an "irritant" if necessary, to stir him to action.

An age-old but most effective way of providing the kind of pupil stimulation we are talking about is to ask questions. Though it is not the province of this book to treat all teaching methods in detail, the discussion that follows (on questions and answers) is included because it is specially related to the view of the teacher as an implanter. Perhaps there are other methods which also have this special relationship, but they are not as conspicuous in the ministry of Jesus. Group discussion, for example, is a fine modern method with special power to stimulate pupils. However, if Jesus used it to any considerable extent, the account is missing from the gospels. (This may be because the gospels are much more concerned about recording the words of Jesus than the words of others who may have made comments in His presence.)

JESUS AND QUESTIONS

Socrates had made the question-and-answer method famous even before the time of Christ. But neither Socrates nor any other teacher was ever able to probe as deep and skillfully into the heart of man as did Jesus. So in this, as we have in other skills useful to us as teachers, let us look at the way our Master treated the subject.

The gospels report more than a hundred instances where Jesus made use of questions. If we go through His ministry and identify the various techniques He used, questions are numerically at the top. This does not mean He spent more *time* asking questions than doing anything else, for a question can be quite brief and a parable quite long. But it does mean that asking questions was certainly a favorite technique of His. Perhaps it is significant that the first recorded words of Jesus were in the form of a question: "Wist ye not that I must be about my Father's business?" (Luke 2:49).

Jesus' questions were of many different types, and therefore could be analyzed many different ways. Here are three observations concerning them that will suggest how you can make your own questions to your class like the ones Jesus asked as He taught.

STIMULATE

1. *Jesus' questions were more to stimulate than to get answers.* Here He was following His own Father's example, for Jehovah's first question of the entire Bible, "Adam . . . where art thou?" (Genesis 3:9), was asked not because God needed to know, but because *Adam* needed to know—to recognize his fallen position. Likewise God's second question (Genesis 4:9), "Where is Abel thy brother?" was not a quest for information; God had the information. He was seeking to stir the conscience, to arouse Cain to recognize what he had done.

Likewise Jesus asked His questions largely to make men think and feel. "Tell me therefore, which of them will love him most?" (Luke 7:42) is one example. Another is "Shall he not much more clothe you?" (Matthew 6:30).

Some of Jesus' questions were of the kind we call "rhetorical"—for which no answer was really expected. Others were what we call "leading" questions—whose very form suggests the answer expected. Still others were "dilemma" questions, any answer to which would lead to another question more difficult or even impossible to answer. An example is found in Matthew 21:25: "The baptism of John, whence was it? from heaven, or of men?" The context explains why His listeners were afraid to answer.

Almost invariably the Master's questions were to stir response, not just to get "correct" answers. He did little if any questioning just as a test or examination of His listeners.

To put this principle in modern terms you as a teacher can use, think of it this way. *Ask questions that will require subjective answers; avoid those to which only objective answers are possible.* By a subjective answer we mean one which can be answered by the pupil from his own opinion or experience. By an objective answer we mean one of fact in which opinion is of minor importance. "Who killed Goliath?" is a question calling for an objective answer. "Who is your favorite Old Testament character?" is a question calling for a subjective answer.

Of course it would be far too extreme to say that objective answers should never be called for. But if you stick to that kind of question you may soon be getting little more than a parrot-like response from your class. Or, perhaps worse, you may be getting no response at all. For when a pupil feels unsure of himself he will be afraid to volunteer to answer a right-or-wrong type of question. But if you ask him for his *opinion* about something, how can his answer be wrong? It can't, for he is obviously the world's best authority on his own opinions. So he can answer with confidence.

Use your questions to stimulate, to get response, to provoke thought and expression, not to fish for a predetermined answer. Remember that when it comes to questions, it is really not too important for the *teacher* to get his answer. What is important is that the pupil be helped to find answers to *his* (the pupil's own) questions.

PERSONALIZE

2. *Jesus' questions were more personalized than general.* It is amazing how many of them were filled with second person pronouns. Notice a few from among many:

"Why beholdest thou the mote that is in thy brother's eye, but considerest not the beam that is in thine own eye?" (Matthew 7:3).

"What went ye out into the wilderness to see?" (Matthew 11:7).

"Which of you shall have . . . an ox . . . and will not . . . pull him out on the sabbath day?" (Luke 14:5, 6).

"Which of you by taking thought can add one cubit unto his stature?" (Matthew 6:27).

He could have put into his questions "some man" or "what person" or "suppose somebody. . . ." But He used instead words like "thou," "thee," "you," "ye." In this way His questions not only stirred His listeners to think about the truth, but to think about the truth *in relation to themselves,* which is more to the point. It is noticeable that He used these specific pronouns a greater proportion of the time in His questions than He did in His straight declarative statements. Could it be because He recognized that a question prods the listener to make his own application, whereas a statement implies you are making the application for him?

In the final analysis, Christian truth is only of benefit as each individual applies it to himself; no one else can do it for him. We reject the idea that singing a certain song, reading a certain verse, or kneeling in a certain position are of any magical importance in themselves. The vital ingredient is the attitude of the individual. Questions to your class, personalized to the individuals concerned (though not necessarily calling names), are a powerful means of bringing about the changed attitudes that are the true measure of learning.

BE PRACTICAL

3. *Jesus' questions were more practical than sophisticated.* It was for others to ask about such highly hypothetical matters as the resurrection status of a much-married woman (Matthew 22:28). Jesus stuck to real life situations, easily pictured, quickly grasped. "If the salt have lost his savour, wherewith shall it be salted?" (Matthew 5:13).

A good question should always make the truth *more* real, never *less* real. Therefore avoid using those which sound fictional or too complex. We smile at the stories about how medieval churchmen wasted time on questions like "How many angels could dance on the head of a pin?" Yet whenever we ourselves ask questions the answers to which require complicated gymnastics of logic or scriptural interpretation, we may be equally guilty of giving people the impression that religion is mostly theoretical after all. This can be true even when the question is of genuine importance. (An example might be "Will Jesus come back to earth before the year 2000?")

THE PUPIL AS QUESTIONER

We usually think of a teaching method as being strictly a tool of the teacher himself. Yet many such a tool may also be used consciously or unconsciously by the pupil as he learns. This is particularly true of the question method. That is, the teaching-learning process takes place not only through questions asked by the teacher, but also through those asked by the pupil. Your questions, if they really begin to succeed in reaching deep, will in turn provoke questions. When this happens, take heart; there is no more sure sign you are doing your job well.

When a pupil has a sincerely questioning mind, he is in just the right attitude to learn. It is then that some of your best teaching can take place. Be careful not to shun or cut off questions just because they may make you uneasy and uncomfortable. Of *course* you are uncomfortable! The questioning student creates just the kind of situation that is least under your control. You never know what questions the class will come up with next. You never feel totally prepared. You must think on your feet.

So, despite its opportunities, the question asked by a pupil may stir small, unconscious resentments within you. Be cautious lest with a condescending smile or an impatient tone of voice you seem to say, "I can't understand how *this* question can be bothering anyone." It is a good rule never to let yourself react with shock—or even surprise—no matter what you are asked. This way you will keep the lines of communication always open. Pupils will learn you are the kind of teacher they can talk to. In the process they may deliberately throw some startling questions at you just to test you. If you pass, they'll start asking about what's *really* on their minds.

ANSWER WHEN?

The idea of a "question period" at the end of a class session is usually unrealistic. It may look nice on a teacher's lesson plan sheet, but will hardly ever work well with a small group. A question, after all, arises because of a problem, great or small, in the mind of a pupil. It is a natural momentary interruption in the learning process, yet vital to that process. In this sense a question is like the rung of a ladder: it is a means of progress, yet of itself it is actually a temporary stopping point. The best time to deal with a question is when it arises. And the best time to have it arise is when it is born in the mind of the individual pupil. For him to try to hold it in abeyance may make him miss or give only superficial attention to other material being presented.

To use a further simile, a question is something like a hurdle on a race track. The time to cope with it is when you come to it. You can hardly expect to save up all the hurdles and deal with them only at the end of the run. It is best to make clear to your pupils that questions are welcome at any time.

EVALUATING PUPIL QUESTIONS

If a group of pupils were mature enough, it could actually steer its own learning simply by asking questions in the right sequence. This is the sort of thing a missionary has to do when learning an unwritten language where no qualified teacher is available. But in the Sunday school classroom it is rarely feasible or necessary for pupil questions to have a place of such overwhelming importance. Here your basic problem (if you have gotten as far as stimulating some questions) is the matter of how much class time they are worth. Such considerations as the following may help you decide.

1. *How broad is the concern the question manifests?* The questions worth the most time are usually those that have been bothering a number of people, even though perhaps expressed by just one. Class members may be impatient about time spent on some question with which they can feel no personal identification.

2. *How deep is the concern the question manifests?* If it is truly urgent in the sense of being about a

real-life, in-progress struggle the questioner is facing, it is probably worth considerable time and effort, even if it doesn't concern the whole class. This kind of question should never be slighted; but it may sometimes be better answered in private.

3. *How is the concern of the question related to the particular area of truth being studied?* If it is in the mainstream of your prepared thoughts, it is easy and logical to give it full treatment. If it is too far off the subject, you may want to answer it only briefly. However, you should face the fact that occasionally a question will arise that is so important in terms of considerations 1 and 2 above that it deserves full attention even though it is off your intended subject. Naturally, it is a teacher's hope that the questions he is asked will be in the field of his competence and preparation. But even a disruption of planned curriculum may be worthwhile if it is in response to thoughtful questions the answering of which will bring spiritual and intellectual growth.

WHAT SHAPE ANSWERS?

Once you have made an evaluation of a pupil's question (a process which must usually be done within a second or two of hearing it), what form should your answer take? Firm rules are difficult to make, for so much depends upon the variables of the who, what, when, where, and why of the question. There is hardly a single characteristic which the answers of Jesus show consistently in *every* instance. Some were short, some long; some sharp, some mild. A dozen other such contrasts could be listed. But there are a few observations possible which clearly apply to *most* of the answers He gave.

1. *Jesus gave answers that led on to more truth, more thought, more discovery by the pupil.* When He was asked, "What shall I do to inherit eternal life?" (Luke 10:25) His answer was, "What is written in the law?" This technique of answering a question with a question was one He used often. But even His declarative answers contained the same quality, leading the pupil on. The question, "Who then can be saved?" brought the reply, "The things . . . impossible with men are possible with God" (Luke 18:27). Hardly ever did He use an answer to *terminate* a line of thought, but rather to push it further.

2. *Jesus gave answers that contained concrete illustration.* "Who is my neighbour?" (Luke 10:29) evoked the story of the good Samaritan. Since we have already considered this characteristic style in our consideration of His whole approach to teaching, we need not reiterate its values again as part of these particular observations about His answers.

3. *Jesus gave answers that were aimed at the questioner, not merely at the question.* He replied to the attitude and the motive rather than to just the words. When Peter asked Him, "What shall this man do?" (John 21:21) His answer did not speak to the semantics of the question at all, but only to the curiosity which prompted it. On occasion He even answered inaudible questions (Luke 5:22). He sought always to answer man's need for *heart* satisfaction rather than his wish for *verbal* satisfaction.

THE HUMAN QUESTION

Here we are very close to the center of your truest function as a teacher: You must answer the *pupil*, not merely his questions. There are answers to be given to the demands of the curriculum, the time schedule, the methods you employ. But the biggest pull of all is the question composed of the total pupil himself. His very presence in your class is a question, a living, human question seeking answers.

You cannot *hand* your pupils satisfactory solutions to life's problems; you cannot *impart* prefabricated answers. But you can *implant* values, principles, keys that will help them find answers for themselves in God and His Word. You can so teach as to be able to share the words of the Master as His own teaching neared its end (John 17:8, 12, 26) : "I have given unto them the words which thou gavest me ... While I was with them in the world, I kept them ... And I have declared unto them thy name, and will declare it. . . . "

QUESTIONS

1. Is it possible for a teacher to cause a pupil to learn beyond the teacher's own level?

2. Explain the sense in which a teacher's efforts are "amplified" in the lives of his pupils.

3. Is it always wrong for a teacher to start what he can't finish?

4. Whose questions are more important to have answered, the pupil's or the teacher's?

5. For what purpose does a teacher ask questions?

6. What were some general characteristics of Jesus' questions?

7. How are pupil questions a good sign?

8. What considerations help a teacher evaluate a pupil's question in terms of how much time should be devoted to answering it?

9. What were some general characteristics of Jesus' answers to questions?

10. What is meant by "answering the *questioner*, not just the *question*"?

BOOKS FOR FURTHER STUDY

Barton, Bruce, *The Man Nobody Knows,* Indianapolis: Bobbs-Merrill, 1925 (new edition 1962).

Calkins, Raymond, *How Jesus Dealt with Men,* New York: Abingdon-Cokesbury, 1942.

Curtis, William A., *Jesus Christ the Teacher,* London: Oxford University Press, 1943.

Edge, Findley B., *Teaching for Results,* Nashville: Broadman Press, 1956.

Horne, Herman H., *Jesus the Master Teacher,* New York: Association Press, 1934.

LeBar, Lois E., *Education That Is Christian,* Westwood, N. J.: Fleming H. Revell, 1958.

Lever, Katherine, *The Perfect Teacher,* New York: Seabury Press, 1964.

Price, J. M., *Jesus the Teacher,* Nashville: Convention Press, 1946.